A PRACTICAL GUIDE TO
ASSET PROTECTION

Bud Lethbridge
Blair R. Jackson, M.A., J.D.
G. James Christiansen, J.D.

IMPORTANT DISCLOSURE - PLEASE READ THIS!

We are dedicating this book, to the Mali Rising Foundation.

Mali Rising Foundation is a small and growing group of people in the United States who have become so impressed with the hope for a brighter future for Mali's children that they are dedicated to building hundreds of schools throughout that nation. The Foundation has just begun to create educational opportunities with the 15 schools it has built in just the last few years, and more being planned.

The Mali Rising Foundation is a non-profit organization established to provide better access to education for millions of children in Mali and around the world. The Foundation's goal is to increase significantly the literacy rate among individuals and communities in underdeveloped nations. Mali Rising Foundation works in partnership with the Malian people and Government. The villages donate the land and furnishes much of the labor. The government provides the teachers.

Together, they have built 15 schools hosting more than 1000 students every year. All of the schools are functioning without likelihood of future funding from Mali Rising Foundation. These schools are proudly owned and operated by villagers, and will provide educational opportunities for many generations of students.

So with all the charities and organizations out there doing good, we love the idea of empowering people, and in this case a whole nation. Putting them in a position to "do" for themselves! We have checked this organization out, met the principals, and are convinced it is a cause worth fighting for and working for. That's why we have aligned ourselves with this wonderful group, and are bringing attention, revenue and our own efforts to the table.

We invite you to go to www.malirisingfoundation.org to find out more about them, to donate, and to see how you can get involved in making a difference!!

Enthusiastically,

Bud, Blair, and James

Table of Contents

Introduction

The world of asset protection planning is fluid and dynamic, constantly impacted by federal and state legislation, judicial interpretation, public policy shifts, revised courtroom rules and procedures, and politics. Further, for those who venture offshore, asset protection planning is often influenced by volatile political changes, revolutions, natural disasters, and unstable economies. Because asset protection planning can present a moving target, good advisors will counsel you to have your plans reviewed and updated from time to time.

Our intention with this book is to provide an overview of many different concepts and tools which may be used in developing your first asset protection plan or updating your existing plan. Since this book presents a general overview, we recognize some techniques may or may not be applicable to your individual needs. We do hope, however, that this overview will educate you on a myriad of available opportunities.

As you put these concepts and ideas into practice, we cannot overemphasize the importance of using competent and licensed professionals, who are trained and prepared to help you implement these concepts into workable action plans. We advise those in need of tax planning strategies to seek out practicing and experienced, certified public accountants (CPAs). Likewise, worthwhile and reliable asset protection plans are best accomplished with the guidance and help of licensed and practicing asset protection attorneys. It is never a bad idea to consult with CPAs and attorneys located in your own state. Please seek these professionals when preparing and implementing your asset protection plan.

We hope the ideas and techniques presented in this book will give you a general framework to start with an asset protection plan. In fact, we hope our book will be read by individuals seeking to protect their assets, and by practicing professional accountants and attorneys who will help facilitate the process.

Further, asset protection planning requires much more than creating paperwork or making some filings with your Secretary of State's office. Unfortunately, we frequently see asset protection plans start and end with entity creation. We hope to impress upon you that achieving the ultimate goals of your asset protection plan will require diligence and care from inception to end. Additionally, implementation of an asset protection plan should impact how you conduct both your personal and your professional life.

Although we do not intend to cast doubt on any particular asset protection "gurus," we feel it would be irresponsible not to provide a gentle warning. We often see the latest and greatest planning firm touting what they believe is a foolproof asset protection strategy. Many times these firms claim to know the latest strategy of moving assets into a safe and secure location while reducing or eliminating liability. Sometimes, they go as far as to claim that, in the process, they can nearly eliminate your taxes. What's more, they suggest all of this can be done for about the same cost as a used Honda! While a good asset protection plan can provide great protection for your assets, depending on the situation, it is not feasible to protect 100% of your assets and not pay certain taxes all of the time. All too often, these offerings are simply not what they promise.

Be careful to choose attorneys and accountants who have experience in this area and have your best interests at heart.
We hope you enjoy this book and find it worthwhile in your pursuit of asset protection.

Sincerely,

Bud, Blair, and James

Chapter 1

What is Asset Protection?

W e are often asked to define the term "asset protection." Clearly, there are many answers. Broadly defined, the term "asset" means anything useful, desirable, or having exchange value. Consequently, the definition of the term "asset protection" is equally broad. For example, removing your keys from your car when you leave it unattended is a good way to protect your asset. Locking it is even better. Likewise, putting your money into a bank account or a safety deposit box is safer than keeping it in a shoebox under your bed. These activities are technically "asset protection."

In this book, we are not going to address the myriad of ways to protect assets. Instead, we will explain several basic strategies to protect your assets, legally. Notice, we use the term "legal." Anyone who would advocate "illegal" means for asset protection will lead you to more problems than the protection you actually seek. Therefore, our concepts and strategies are based upon safe, legal applications. These concepts include considering estate planning tools, business formation and governance, real estate and property laws, insurance, bankruptcy, contracts, and others. As we consider these concepts, we should not lose sight of the ultimate goal: minimize risk and protect your assets.

Due to the litigious society in which we live, we must also consider how our asset protection plan can protect us from potential lawsuits. We call this our "pre-litigation" strategy. From our perspective, the implementation of pre-litigation strategies is no different from the implementation of the legal concepts mentioned above. Unfortunately, too many of us fail to prepare for a lawsuit, weeks, months, and even years, before it potentially comes. This, in our opinion, is a mistake. The number of attorneys in the United States is staggering. The American Bar Association reported in 2010 that there are over 760,000 practicing attorneys in the United States. Further, on a per capita basis, the United States has more attorneys than any other country in the world, and make no mistake, this army of attorneys is very busy! The State Court Guide to Statistical Reporting estimated over 16 million cases filed in State Courts in 2010. That does not include Federal Court cases. It also does not include cases that were never filed, but likely settled outside of court.

Because there are so many attorneys and filed lawsuits, the impact of this litigation is far reaching and affects everyone to some extent. Our recommendation is that individuals implement a pre-litigation strategy in the same manner they would prepare for a potential natural disaster. Both are possible to predict, and wreak total devastation if we are unprepared. For example, if you live in an area prone to earthquakes, it makes sense to protect yourself against an earthquake, i.e., insurance covering damages caused by earthquakes, retaining walls, earthquake sustainable foundations, etc. If you run a business, you risk the potential of being sued by a supplier, employee, competitor, etc. There are ways to protect your personal assets from such litigation, so you are prepared when the disaster strikes.

A central component of a pre-litigation strategy is to create a paper foxhole. In battle, we know that a foxhole will protect us from enemy assault by digging in and surrounding ourselves with defenses. The same applies with a pre-litigation strategy. We can retain documents, which in effect, will become our defenses. These papers will protect us from the harm that lurks down the road in the form of a lawsuit. For example, proper corporate minutes will ensure the entity under which you are conducting business is not set aside, so a creditor may attempt to collect from you personally. A proper corporate shell with documentation will provide much asset protection, if well documented.

Furthermore, anyone who has ever been involved in a court proceeding, whether it was in a small claims court or a trial before a federal district court, knows the most important factor in winning in court is being able to tell and prove your side of the story. Attorneys who represent individuals and businesses in court proceedings are called litigators, and top litigators are the best storytellers. The most effective way you can help those litigators is to retain good evidence and give them accurate facts to establish your case or defense. In short, one way to protect your assets is to document your story long before a case is filed against you. This will allow you to present your story long before it becomes an actual issue.

We cannot over-emphasize the documentation aspect of your story. Even the best memories fade and details and facts are not retained if you do not document your actions. Our experience has also taught us that judges and juries are much more likely to rely upon documented facts versus oral recitations of what occurred. You must maintain complete, accurate, and if necessary, signed documentation to ensure your protection.

In summary, we intend to present a high-level overview of concepts and legal theories, which you may implement in your asset protection plan, to give you peace of mind. Hopefully, by considering the ideas presented herein, you will be better prepared to embark on a process that will serve you and your family for years to come.

Chapter 2

An Overview of Estate Planning

Some attorneys believe "estate planning" is different from "asset protection," and thus, should be considered separately. We disagree. In our experience, planning to protect assets without thinking about your estate is problematic. For example, consider a case where you transfer all of your real property into joint tenancy[1]. If you later execute a will, that will cannot bequeath the property to another because you have no right in the property after death. Consequently, if you adopt an asset protection plan that puts all of your real property into joint tenancy, and you later execute a will believing you can devise the property amongst your children, regardless of the order of passing of the joint tenants, you will be mistaken. Likewise, if you place certain property into an irrevocable trust as an asset protection strategy, when creating the trust, you must consider how property within the trust will be transferred at death. It is important to view asset protection in conjunction with your estate plan to ensure the two are compatible and do not create any inconsistencies.

It should go without saying that many of the concepts that apply to asset protection planning apply to estate planning and vice versa. This makes sense because of the many overlapping issues involved with estate and asset protection plans. As a result, we have included a

---

[1]Joint tenancy differs from a tenancy in common because each joint tenant has a right of survivorship to the other's share. BLACK LAW DICTIONARY, Third Pocket Edition, pg. 709. Under joint tenancy, if there are two "tenants," both tenants have equal access to the property. If one tenant dies, then his share goes to the surviving joint tenant. Joint tenancy trumps the dead tenant's will because he did not have the right to give the property to another after death.

brief overview of estate planning in this chapter. The estate planning concepts identified in this chapter could easily be the subject matter of the entire book; indeed, volumes of books exist on this topic. For the sake of brevity, we will not address each concept in detail, but will discuss general principles that will give you a greater understanding of how an estate plan may work in conjunction with your asset protection plan. These concepts will set the stage for you to have a more in-depth conversation with an estate-planning attorney in your state of residence. Each concept should be considered with the advice of a qualified professional.

Intestate Succession

Have you ever asked yourself these questions?

> *What happens to my assets at death?*
> *Do I have to plan as to how my estate will be divided?*
> *Is it necessary to have a will?*
> *If I do not have a will, where will my assets go?*
> *When I die, do my creditors get paid?*
> *Can my creditors make a claim on my estate?*
> *Are there ways to protect my assets by planning ahead?*

The answers to these questions depend on how you planned for, or did not plan for, your death.

First, we will address the situation where you die without a will. This is called dying intestate. Most states have enacted intestacy laws that dictate where your property goes should you die without a will. The intestacy laws are usually applied in probate court— a special court designed to deal with the transfer of assets at death.

Intestacy laws are designed to apply the fairest standards possible, as determined by the legislatures in each of the states, to the masses. For example, under some state laws, if you are married and have no children when you die, all of your estate will go to your surviving spouse. If you are married and have children that survive you, your surviving spouse is entitled to a certain dollar amount, plus one-half of the balance of the intestacy estate. If one or more of your surviving descendants is not a descendant of your surviving spouse, then it falls under another set of guidelines.

What this means is, if you and your spouse have children together and you have no children outside of your marriage at the time of your death, then your surviving spouse will receive everything. If your surviving spouse is not a parent of your children, then the surviving spouse will receive a certain sum plus one-half of the balance of the estate; the other half of the estate will be divided between your children. Most state statutes go into great detail as to what happens if you have no surviving spouse and what happens if you have no children. Because you might be killed in a car accident where others are injured, some states intestacy laws require heirs to survive the decedent's death for more than one hundred and twenty hours.

Many attorneys have regularly counseled individuals who have little or no assets that they do not require a will, since the value of their assets does not merit a decision as to where their assets go. In other circumstances, attorneys and clients will review the intestacy laws of their state and some individuals will decide they are comfortable with the provisions contained in the intestacy laws.

However, relying completely on intestacy laws is problematic. First, like all laws, intestacy laws evolve and change. The time, cost, and effort to stay up to date with intestacy laws is more costly than retaining an attorney to draft a will. Second, change in personal life is inevitable. Divorce, relocation to a new state, adoption, and the death of a child, all affect the distribution of your assets under intestacy. Lastly, people die unexpectedly. Car accidents, disease, and natural disasters are hard to predict. Consequently, the untimely death of a parent, child, or spouse, could significantly affect your estate's distribution.

As stated above, you may pass your assets at death without a will or a trust. In some circumstances, the applicable intestacy laws will provide a workable and acceptable resolution. For many years, intestacy laws varied dramatically from state to state. In 1969, several scholars collaborated and produced what they considered the fairest and best guidelines for distributing assets at death. The guidelines were intended to become a set of uniform intestacy laws to provide consistency across the country. The work was entitled the Uniform Probate Code (UPC). Because of these scholars and authors work, approximately one-third of the states adopted some or all of the UPC.

Since 1969, the UPC has undergone several revisions, including significant changes in 1989, the 1990s, and 2006. Some states adopted the revisions while others did not. Interestingly, a few states adopted portions of the amended UPC, without adopting the original. Because the UPC dominates the landscape as a general overview of intestacy laws, it is worthy of consideration. However, as stated before, these guidelines may or may not be applicable in your state.

A few provisions of the UPC are worthy of attention: Section 2-101 (general definition of intestacy), 2-102 (the share of a surviving spouse under intestacy), 2-103 (the remaining share after the surviving spouse has taken their portion), and 2-105 (what happens if no beneficiary of your estate exists). The following sections in their entirety are set forth below[2].

---

[2] Noteworthy details: the distribution of assets under intestacy requires the estate to go through probate. Probate is a state court action where a judge will distribute the estate pursuant to the local intestacy statute. There is a fee for probate. The fee varies by jurisdiction and can equal a percentage of the estate or be a flat fee. Because probate is complicated, it typically requires an attorney. Thus, one of the biggest detriments to probate is the extra cost it takes from the estate. Depending on the circumstances, probate is very expensive.

Uniform Probate Code (2006)

Section 2 101— Intestate Estate

(1.) Any part of a decedent's estate not effectively disposed of by will passes by intestate succession to the decedent's heirs as prescribed in this Code, except as modified by the decedent's will.

(2.) A decedent by will may expressly exclude or limit the right of an individual or class to succeed to property of the decedent passing by intestate succession. If that individual or a member of that class survives the decedent, the share of the decedent's intestate estate to which that individual or class would have succeeded passes as if that individual or each member of that class had disclaimed his [or her] intestate share.

Section 2 102 — Share of Spouse

The intestate share of a decedent's surviving spouse is:

(1) The entire intestate estate if:

(i) No descendant or parent of the decedent survives the decedent; or

(ii) All of the decedent's surviving descendants are also descendants of the surviving spouse and there is no other descendant of the surviving spouse who survives the decedent;

(2) The first [$200,000], plus three fourths of any balance of the intestate estate, if no descendant of the decedent survives the decedent, but a parent of the decedent survives the decedent;

(3) The first [$150,000], plus one half of any balance of the intestate estate, if all of the decedent's surviving descendants

are also descendants of the surviving spouse and the surviving spouse has one or more surviving descendants who are not descendants of the decedent;

(4)   The first [$100,000], plus one half of any balance of the intestate estate, if one or more of the decedent's surviving descendants are not descendants of the surviving spouse.

Section 2 103 — Share of Heirs Other Than Surviving Spouse.

Any part of the intestate estate not passing to the decedent's surviving spouse under Section 2 102, or the entire intestate estate if there is no surviving spouse, passes in the following order to the individuals designated below who survive the decedent:

(1) To the decedent's descendants by representation;

(2) If there is no surviving descendant, to the decedent's p a r e n t s equally if both survive, or to the surviving parent;

(3) If there is no surviving descendant or parent, to the descendants of the decedent's parents or either of them by representation;

(4) If there is no surviving descendant, parent, or descendant of a parent, but the decedent is survived by one or more grandparents or descendants of grandparents, half of the estate passes to the decedent's paternal grandparents equally if both survive, or to the surviving paternal grandparent, or to the descendants of the decedent's paternal grandparents or either of them if both are deceased, the descendants taking by representation; and the other half passes to the decedent's maternal relatives in the same manner; but if there is no surviving grandparent or descendant of a grandparent on either the paternal or the maternal side, the entire estate passes to the decedent's relatives on the other side in the same manner as the half.

Section 2 105 — No Taker

If there is no taker under the provisions of this Article, the intestate estate passes to the [state].

For those interested, the UPC is available online. Your local law school, court, or public library may have physical copies for you to review or access to the Internet[3]. As previously mentioned, there is not enough room in this book to cover all of the sections of the UPC or specific state intestacy laws. Some additional sections you might want to look at include: section 2-110 (estate debts to decedents); section 2-114, (parent child relationships); and section 2-210 (personal liability of beneficiaries). Some readers of

the UPC will undoubtedly find the provisions of it match closely to their wishes. This is not surprising considering the wealth of intellect that has spent years investigating and determining the best interests of the general populace. However, also as previously stated, when you die intestate, you allow the statutes to choose for you. For those who are not comfortable with that plan, they may want to consider a will or a trust.

Last Will & Testament

A will, sometimes called a last will and testament, is a legal declaration made by a person, also known as the "testator." In a will, the testator names one or more persons, companies, entities, or charities who should receive the transfer of his or her property upon the testator's death. These individuals are generally referred to as "beneficiaries." The will also outlines who is to become the "personal representative" of the estate upon the testator's death. A personal representative has the right and responsibility to carry out the wishes of the testator. As discussed below, a will is a very important part of an asset protection and estate plan.

---

[3]Two great online resources include the Law Library of Cornell, found at www.law.cornell.edu and the Law Library of the University of Pennsylvania, found at www.upenn.edu.

For young couples, perhaps the most important provisions of a will pertain to the care of their young children. Although some may disagree during teenage years, children are parents' greatest assets. How children are treated and cared for is a significant part of a will. In particular, in a will you can designate an individual who is responsible for your children upon your untimely death. Usually, this person is called a "guardian." The guardian will watch over your children should something happen to both parents. You can see why a guardian is important. Consider the situation where both mother and father die at the same time and leave children behind. The deceased parents both have living parents (grandparents) who desire to raise the children. Who should win? Unfortunately, there is no easy answer to this question, and ultimately, if the parties cannot decide amongst themselves, the matter will end up in court. Custody battles in court are never pretty and will always have a negative effect on children. Consequently, the designation of a guardian and the existence of a will are vital.

Lest you think a battle over children might not happen in your family, consider the situation above, but this time the mother and father have a two million dollar life insurance policy which is left to the children. While we would hope those who the state appoints as guardians would put the interests of the children first, not all do. A will circumvents this concern by designating a guardian for the children at the time of death. In that regard, it is not only an asset protection strategy, it is a "comfort and peace of mind" strategy.

Will drafting is very State specific. Therefore, you should use an attorney licensed in your state, to assist you in its preparation. It's good to have a basic understanding of what is contained in a will prior to talking to an attorney. This basic knowledge should not circumvent your need to consult with a professional. Rather, it will make the drafting process more efficient as you understand the basic elements that comprise a will.

First, wills must be in writing, witnessed, and signed. For example, some states require you have two witnesses who attest your signing of the will. Other states require you initial each page to ensure you intended the contents of each page be included in your will. The key to remember with formalities is to find out what they are in your state of residence and follow them. Of course, most statutes (laws) contain remedial provisions, which allow you to correct a missed formality. It is always better to adhere to the formalities the first time.

Other common will formalities include clear identification of the maker of the will and that a will is being made. This is sometimes called "publication" of the will. The testator should also declare that he or she has the ability, capacity, and desire to revoke all previous wills. If this is not done, a conflict may arise over different drafts of a will. The easiest and the best way to revoke an old version of a will, is to tear it up. Furthermore, the testator should demonstrate that he or she has the capacity to dispose of his or her property and does so freely and willingly. Practitioners often refer to this as the "Sound Mind" clause. Incapacity is one of the most frequent challenges to the validity of a will. Thus, it is better to execute a will now, than to wait until later, in the case something happens to affect your mental capacity.

Second, one of the benefits of a will is your ability to change or modify it. Circumstances change and you may need to amend or modify your will. Thankfully, when necessary, you can amend and modify it at any time. For this purpose, you may want to review your will periodically. This is especially true when you experience a major life event, like moving to a different state, or when your marital status changes. Further, a will should be reviewed for changes to laws, especially tax laws, from time to time.

Third, although you may amend or update your will, most states have specific rules on how to revoke a will. In some states, you may revoke a will by simply drafting and signing a new one. The presumption in those states is that if you draft and sign a new will, your intention is to revoke the former will. In other states, you must follow the exact formalities to revoke a previously issued (signed) will. Therefore, you may want to consult a local attorney as to your state's testamentary formalities to revoke your will. This is important, not just in case you want to revoke an old will, but also to make sure your actions do not revoke a will you want to keep. In other states, a will may be revoked in writing or by some other physical act, like destroying it or obliterating it. In all states, however, if you orally tell anyone that your will is revoked, that is not sufficient for revocation.

Again, the UPC is a great resource when considering general guidelines for will preparation. It is important to know the UPC is a guideline, which may not apply to your state. A general knowledge of the UPC as it applies to wills is helpful. Some sections of particular concern include section 2-501(who can draft a will); 2-502 (execution of a will); 2-503 (harmless error); section 2-504 (self-proved wills); section 2-505 (witnesses); and section 2-506 (choice of law).

Uniform Probate Code (2006)

Section 2 501 — Who May Make Will

An individual 18 or more years of age who is of sound mind may make a will.

Section 2 502 — Execution; Witnessed Wills; Holographic Wills

(a) Except as provided in subsection (b) and in Sections 2-503, 2-506, and 2-513, a will must be:
  (1) In writing;

  (2) Signed by the testator or in the testator's name by some other individual in the testator's conscious presence and by the testator's direction; and

  (3) Signed by at least two individuals, each of whom signed within a reasonable time after he [or she] witnessed either the signing of the will as
  described in paragraph

(2) or the testator's acknowledgment of that signature or acknowledgment of the will.

(b) A will that does not comply with subsection (a) is valid as a holographic will, whether or not witnessed, if the signature and material portions of the document are in the testator's handwriting.

(c) Intent that the document constitutes the testator's will can be established by extrinsic evidence, including, for holographic wills, portions of the document that are not in the testator's handwriting.

Section 2 503 — Harmless Error

Although a document or writing added upon a document was not executed in compliance with Section 2 502, the document or writing is treated as if it had been executed in compliance with that section if the proponent of the document or writing establishes by clear and convincing evidence that the decedent intended the document or writing to constitute (i) the decedent's will, (ii) a partial or complete revocation of the will, (iii) an addition to or an alteration of the will, or (iv) a partial or complete revival of his [or her] formerly revoked will or of a formerly revoked portion of the will.

Section 2 504 — Self Proved Will

(a) A will may be simultaneously executed, attested, and made self proved, by acknowledgment thereof by the testator and affidavits of the witnesses, each made before an officer authorized to administer oaths under the laws of the state in which execution occurs and evidenced by the officer's certificate, under official seal, in substantially the following form:

I, _____, the testator, sign my name to this instrument this _____ day of _____, and being first duly sworn, do hereby declare to the undersigned authority that I sign and execute this instrument as my will and that I sign it willingly (or willingly direct another to sign for me), that I execute it as my free and voluntary act for the purposes

therein expressed, and that I am eighteen years of age or older, of sound mind, and under no constraint or undue influence. _____
Testator
We,_____,_____, the witnesses, sign our names to this instrument, being first duly sworn, and do hereby declare to the undersigned authority that the testator signs and executes this instrument as [his] [her] will and that [he] [she] signs it willingly (or willingly directs another to sign for [him] [her]), and that each of us, in the presence and hearing of the testator, hereby signs this will as witness to the testator's signing, and that to the best of our knowledge the testator is eighteen years of age or older, of sound mind, and under no constraint or undue influence.

_____ Witness
_____ Witness
The State of _____
County of _____

Subscribed, sworn to and acknowledged before me by _____, the testator, and subscribed and sworn to before me by _____, and _____, witnesses, this ____ day of _____.
(Seal) _____(Signed) _____

(b) An attested will may be made self proved at any time after its execution by the acknowledgment thereof by the testator and the affidavits of the witnesses, each made before an officer authorized to administer oaths under the laws of the state in which the acknowledgment occurs and evidenced by the officer's certificate, under the official seal, attached or annexed to the will in substantially the following form:
The State of _____
County of _____
We, _____, _____, and _____, the testator and the witnesses, respectively, whose names are signed to the attached or foregoing instrument, being first duly sworn, do hereby declare to the undersigned

authority that the testator signed and executed the instrument as the testator's will and that [he] [she] had signed willingly (or willingly directed another to sign for [him] [her]), and that [he] [she] executed it as [his] [her] free and voluntary act for the purposes therein expressed, and that each of the witnesses, in the presence and hearing of the testator, signed the will as witness and that to the best of [his] [her] knowledge the testator was at that time eighteen years or age or older, of sound mind, and under no constraint or undue influence.

_____
Testator

_____
Witness

_____
Witness

Subscribed, sworn to and acknowledged before me by _____, the testator, and subscribed and sworn to before me by _____, and _____, witnesses, this ____, day of _____.

(Seal)   (Signed)

_____   _____

_____
(Official capacity of officer)

(c) A signature affixed to a self proving affidavit attached to a will is considered a signature affixed to the will, if necessary to prove the will's due execution.

Section 2 505 — Who May Witness

(a) An individual generally competent to be a witness may act as a witness to a will.

(b) The signing of a will by an interested witness does not invalidate the will or any provision of it.

Section 2 506 — Choice of Law as to Execution

A written will is valid if executed in compliance with Section 2 502 or 2 503 or if its execution complies with the law at the time of execution of the place where the will is executed, or of the law of the place where at the time of execution or at the time of death the testator is domiciled, has a place of abode, or is a national.

Reading sections of the UPC is an excellent way to prepare to draft your own will, as it will identify potential areas of discussion with your attorney. As mentioned above, the UPC is available online. Many law libraries provide free access to it, and any popular search engine will enable you to find it. [4]

Will Substitutes

Wills and intestacy laws are not the only way to transfer assets at death. Over the years, several will substitutes and non-probate transfers have developed that are equally important as estate planning strategies and asset protection strategies.

The most common type of will substitute is life insurance. Life insurance is a contract between a policy owner, typically an individual, and an insurer. The policy owner buys a designated amount of coverage from the insurer, who, upon the policy owner's death, will pay the amount of coverage to a selected beneficiary. Life insurance allows a person to transfer an asset paid for during his or her lifetime, to another after his passing.

Life insurance is just one of several types of non-probate options available. Again, the UPC provides a good, general overview of some of these will substitutes. Of particular interest is section 6-101 (non-probate transfers on death).

---

[4] Two great online resources include the Law Library of Cornell, found at www.law.cornell.edu and the Law Library of the University of Pennsylvania, found at www.upenn.edu.

Section 6 101 — Non-probate Transfers On Death

A provision for a non-probate transfer on death in an insurance policy, contract of employment, bond, mortgage, promissory note, certificated or un-certificated security, account agreement, custodial agreement, deposit agreement, compensation plan, pension plan, individual retirement plan, employee benefit plan, trust, conveyance, deed of gift, marital property agreement, or other written instrument of a similar nature is non-testamentary. This subsection includes a written provision that:

(1) Money or other benefits due to, controlled by, or owned by a decedent before death must be paid after the decedent's death to a person whom the decedent designates either in the instrument or in a separate writing, including a will, executed either before or at the same time as the instrument, or later;

(2) Money due or to become due under the instrument ceases to be payable in the event of death of the promisee or the promisor before payment or demand; or

(3) Any property controlled by or owned by the decedent before death which is the subject of the instrument passes to a person the decedent designates either in the instrument or in a separate writing, including a will, executed either before or at the same time as the instrument, or later.

Tenancies as a Will Substitute

Your personal tenancies may also act as a will substitute. For example, the way you own real property may act as a will substitute. Property held in joint tenancy or tenancy by the entirety passes without the cost or delay of probating your property. In this type of ownership, at the death of one joint tenant or tenant by the entirety, the survivor owns the property absolutely, freed of any participation by the decedent. The theory is that the decedent's interest vanishes at death and therefore, no probate is necessary. An overview of some of the features of a joint tenancy is worthwhile.

First, the creation of a joint tenancy in land gives the joint tenants equal interests upon creation. A person who transfers land into a joint tenancy, cannot, during life, revoke the transfer and cancel the interest given the other joint tenant. This is an example of how joint tenancy works. Consider the following:

> A man and a woman in their early sixties get married. Both were previously married, and both have children from their prior marriages. After their marriage, the man and woman purchase a marital home as joint-tenants. Years later, the woman becomes ill. While under heavy sedation and at the prodding of her children, she signs a deed of trust to her children, transferring her rights to the marital home to them. She dies first and then the man dies. The man has a will devising the marital home to his children. Who has a rightful claim to the property?

The answer to the question is the man's children. Depending upon whether you are the progeny of the man or the woman, you either like or dislike the benefits of joint tenancy.

Second, a joint tenant cannot devise his or her share by will. Perhaps you are wondering how this can be, when in the example above, the man willed the marital home to his children. Let us explain. As stated above, under the "vanishing theory," the property interest of the decedent disappears upon her death, leaving the entire interest to the surviving tenant, in this case, the man. The man receives full ownership, and he may transfer his interest by will or another method. In other words, the woman relinquished her tenancy at death to the man and the man simultaneously no longer holds the property as a joint tenant with her. Because the man takes complete control, he is not devising a tenancy property by will, but rather a property that he holds alone.

The third important feature of joint tenancy is creditor's rights. To satisfy the debt of one tenant against a property held in joint tenancy, the creditor must seize the asset during the joint tenant's life. If not, at death, the joint tenant's interest vanishes and there is nothing for the creditor to reach. Therefore, creditors generally cannot seize property held by the joint tenant who has passed. As you can see, ownership in joint tenancy can be a powerful asset protection device.

A "tenancy by the entirety" is slightly different from a joint tenancy. A tenancy by the entirety is a method of holding real property, available only to married couples[5]. It shares common factors with joint tenancies, in that there must be unity in time, title, interest, and possession, but generally adds the fifth element of marriage. Not all states recognize tenancy by the entirety. Where recognized, there are many benefits. One benefit includes the ability to shield the property from creditors of one spouse. This also applies to bankruptcy relief when only one spouse is filing.

Perhaps the most popular feature of tenancy by the entirety is the ability to extinguish liens. If a non-debtor spouse survives a debtor spouse, a creditor cannot enforce a lien against the property. In other words, the non-debtor spouse takes the property free and clear. On the other hand, if the debtor spouse survives, then the creditor can enforce the lien against the entire property. When considering this type of asset protection strategy, you should hedge against the healthier party!

Revocable Living Trusts as a Will Substitute

A revocable living trust, also known as a revocable inter vivos trust, is the foundation for estate planning strategies and overall asset protection. These trusts have come into widespread use, particularly among the moderately and very wealthy. A revocable living trust is the most flexible of all will substitutes because the donor can draft the dispositive provisions and the administration provisions precisely to the donor's liking.

Under the typical revocable living trust involving a deed of trust, the trust settlor transfers legal title to property to another person as trustee, pursuant to a writing in which the settlor retains the power to

---

[5] Vermont and Hawaii allow domestic partners to own property as tenants by the entirety.

revoke, alter, or amend the trust, and the right to trust income during their lifetime. On the settlor's death, the trust assets are distributed to or held in further trust for other beneficiaries. In the context of asset protection, a revocable living trust can serve multiple purposes:

1) It can reduce estate taxes
2) It can preserve your privacy
3) It can help you to avoid probate
4) It can help you manage your family's financial affairs

A revocable living trust must be established while you are alive. It is revocable, meaning you can make changes whenever you desire, and revoke the trust completely should you need (or want) to in the future. It also allows you to be the trustee of the trust and have complete control during your lifetime, while giving you the ability to choose to whom your assets are distributed in the event of your death.

Many people choose to have a trust because it allows their heirs to avoid probate. As explained above, probate is the legal process of transferring the ownership of property after someone dies. A simple way to tell if you need to go through probate is if you need someone's signature to transfer an asset, and they are no longer alive. Let's say your grandfather passes away and owns a car. The car is titled in your grandfather's name. In order to transfer the car, your grandfather would need to sign the title. Since your grandfather is no longer alive, you need to probate the asset in "probate court" in order to get authority to sign the title on his behalf since he has passed away.

When a revocable living trust is in place, the court's permission is not needed to transfer the property out of the deceased person's name. Instead, a trustee, appointed to administer the affairs of the trust, can sign on behalf of the trust.

Initially, in a revocable living trust, the "grantor" or "settlor" of the trust (generally the individual or individuals who created the trust) may also serve as trustee. Once the grantor becomes incapacitated or passes away, a successor trustee is appointed, pursuant to the terms of the trust. This means whoever is next in line signs a document under penalty of perjury that they are the successor trustee of the trust, and then they are able to act in the capacity of the trustee and transfer assets.

Another benefit of the revocable living trust is privacy. Because the trust is not recorded, filed, or published in public, there is no public record of the administration of the estate. Consequently, the estate administrations are completed in an office, and not in court.

The documents that make up the foundation of a proper estate plan are the will, the powers of attorney, and the revocable living trusts established to hold and administer your personal assets. This concludes the next step in an asset protection plan.

Special Trust Types and Their Use in Asset Protection

English influence on American legislation and jurisprudence is well known. One influencing factor came from the rich who continually sought ways to keep property in the name of their children and grandchildren. Not only did they seek to maintain title, but also to safeguard family assets from accident of fortune and mismanagement. The English created two systems to accomplish this goal: one called the fee tail and the other, strict settlement. An in-depth discussion of these devices is not necessary, or possible in this book, but we can say these devices never really took hold in the United States. The influence from English system, however, did materialize into an American iteration, a true ideological descendant, called the "spendthrift trust."

With a spendthrift trust, the beneficiaries cannot voluntarily alienate their interests nor can creditors reach their interests. It is created by imposing a disabling restraint upon the beneficiaries and their creditors. Consider this example:

> A man devises his property to his son in trust to pay the income from his property to his daughter for her life, and upon his daughter's death, the property is to pass to her children. The trust

prohibits the daughter from transferring her life estate. At the same time, the trust protects the daughter's interest from her creditors by not giving the daughter full control of the asset. Through this trust, therefore, the daughter receives a stream of income that she cannot alienate and her creditors cannot reach.

The spendthrift trust is a tremendous tool in estate planning endeavors and asset protection considerations. Most jurisdictions have adopted a version of it. Some states require a specific spendthrift clause in order for it to be a spendthrift trust. This is a document that should be prepared from a licensed attorney practicing in this area of the law.

Pour-Over Wills in Conjunction with Trust Planning

Along with the increasing use of revocable trusts has come the development of the pour-over will. In concept, it is very simple. A man sets up a revocable inter vivos trust naming his son as trustee. The man transfers to his son, as trustee, his stocks and bonds. The man then executes a will devising the remaining assets or "residue" of his estate to his son, as trustee, to hold under the terms of the inter vivos trust. The pour-over by will of probate assets into an inter vivos trust is a useful device, allowing the man to transfer some of his assets inter vivos, and to merge the remainder after his death. Further, the man can merge other assets into the same trust, like insurance proceeds.

The UPC addresses the pour-over will in section 2-511.

Section 2 511 — Testamentary Additions to Trusts

(a) A will may validly devise property to the trustee of a trust established or to be established

(i) During the testator's lifetime by the testator, by the testator and some other person, or by some other person, including a funded or unfunded life insurance trust, although the settlor has reserved any or all rights of ownership of the insurance contracts, or

(ii) At the testator's death by the testator's devise to the trustee, if the trust is identified in the testator's will and its terms are set forth in a written instrument, other than a will, executed before, concurrently with, or after the execution of the testator's will or in another individual's will if that other individual has predeceased the testator, regardless of the existence, size, or character of the corpus of the trust. The devise is not invalid because the trust is amendable or revocable, or because the trust was amended after the execution of the will or the testator's death.

(b) Unless the testator's will provides otherwise, property devised to a trust described in subsection (a) is not held under a testamentary trust of the testator, but it becomes a part of the trust to which it is devised, and must be administered and disposed of in accordance with the provisions of the governing instrument setting forth the terms of the trust, including any amendments thereto made before or after the testator's death.

(c) Unless the testator's will provides otherwise, a revocation or termination of the trust before the testator's death causes the devise to lapse.

Other Considerations in Estate Planning—The Power of Attorney

A power of attorney is a legal document that allows another person to act as the agent for the one who is the principle in the document. Essentially, by signing a power of attorney, you are giving another person permission to act as if they were you. In a general durable power of attorney, most couples will appoint their spouses as their agent, which will allow the other to sign their name as if they were their spouse. This can be very convenient when allowing the transfer of real or other property when one of the spouses is away on business. It can also cause problems when the power is used without the other's knowledge or consent. Power of attorney is a very powerful document that can allow another person to do what they will with your assets. Accordingly, great care should be taken in determining who should be appointed the agent under a power of attorney.

A power of attorney is also what is known as a life document. This means that a power of attorney can only be used while the principle is alive. Once the principle has passed away, the power of attorney is then voided, considering that a power of attorney uses the legal terms of 'principle' and 'agent.'

Other Considerations in Estate Planning—The Healthcare Power of Attorney

Unlike a general, durable power of attorney, the healthcare power of attorney authorizes another individual to make medical decisions on the principle's behalf. This is important because of the passage of the Health Insurance Portability and Accountability Act (HIPAA), which was enacted by the United States Congress in 1996. This law makes your healthcare records private and only under a healthcare power of attorney or other authorized state documents, such as a HIPAA release form, can another person know any information regarding the principle's medical condition, and access vital medical records in order to make an informed decision on the principle's behalf. Again, most couples will elect their spouses to be the initial agent under a healthcare power of attorney to allow them to make medical decisions if the principle is unable to do so.

Other Considerations in Estate Planning—The Healthcare Directive Acts

Healthcare directive acts allow you to appoint another person to make healthcare decisions when you are unable to make those decisions yourself, to record your wishes about healthcare in writing, to change or revoke the healthcare directive and make the directive legal. The healthcare directive allows your appointed agent to consent to, refuse, or withdraw any healthcare, to hire and fire healthcare providers, to get copies of your medical records, obtain consultations and second opinions, ask questions, and get answers from healthcare providers.

Without this document or a healthcare power of attorney as explained above, not even your spouse or parent could obtain information about your medical care, even if you are unconscious or in a coma. Having this and other estate planning documents are essential for your protection and needs.

By far the most famous and prolific health care cases, which could have been entirely prevented by a health care directive, involved a Florida resident named Terri Schiavo. On February 25, 1990, this unfortunate woman suffered from a cardiac arrest which caused her severe brain damage. She later entered a coma and then a vegetative state from which she never recovered. In 1998, her husband petitioned a Florida court to allow the feeding tube keeping her alive to be removed. Terri's parents intervened, and a massive court battle erupted. The argument became so heated that even the United States President, George Bush, had to intervene. Ultimately, after fourteen appeals, five federal lawsuits, and a myriad of other twists and turns which included Florida legislation being struck down by the Florida Supreme Court and the United States Supreme Court being petitioned four different times to intervene, the matter was resolved in 2005. The seventeen-year ordeal, at least for Terri Schiavo, ended on March 31, 2005, when she finally passed away after being removed from life support.

Can you imagine a more impactful situation on a family? Mrs. Schiavo was an insurance clerk, living in an average Florida community. She was not a person of notoriety or wealth. She was an everyday citizen who, because of circumstance outside of her control, was thrown into the national spotlight for seventeen years. From an asset protection perspective, whatever assets she had were surely dissipated in health care costs and legal wrangling.

Chapter **3**

Introduction to Business Entities and an Overview of the Sole Proprietorship

There are several types of business entities and forms where an individual or group of individuals can conduct business. These can include the following:

1) Sole Proprietorship
2) Partnerships, Limited Partnerships, and Limited Liability Partnerships
3) Corporations and their federal tax status of "S" or "C"
4) Limited Liability Companies (LLC)
5) Non-profit Corporations

All business forms are regulated and provided for by state law. Therefore, there is no such thing as a federal company. In order to carry on business in multiple states, you are required to register your entity in each of those states. The term "conducting business" varies from state to state. For example, in some states, owning real property within the state does not mean you are conducting business there. Consequently, if you buy a piece of property in that state, you may not need to register your company there. On the other hand, in some states, if you solicit business in their state by conducting telemarketing, you are required to register your company. Whether or not your business requires registration within the state is determined by how your company conducts its transactions.

Although the federal government does not regulate business entities, it does tax them. Further, various entities are taxed differently. When a person mentions their "S" or "C" corporation, what they are referring to is the way they have designated that their corporation is taxed. Beyond taxation, each type of business form or entity has vastly different asset protection advantages and disadvantages. We hope to highlight in a general fashion what those are.

Sole Proprietorship

A Sole Proprietorship is when an individual goes out into the marketplace and conducts business as him or herself. This is the simplest type of business form and usually does not require any formal requirements to create or operate. Typically, an individual who operates under this business form obtains what is known as a 'Doing Business As' (DBA) license, to comply with city, county, or state licensing requirements. When an individual chooses to do business as a DBA, he or she can do business under a different name. This is normally called a fictitious name, simply because you would not be operating under your own name. Registering a fictitious name is usually a simple process. Forms are readily available for an individual to fill out a fictitious name form and obtain a DBA license. If the business is selling items, then a sales tax, sales tax ID, and a license are usually required.

There is no asset protection advantage to an individual operating a business under a DBA. If the company gets sued, the individual gets sued. Since there is no asset protection or tax benefit whatsoever with a sole proprietorship, most attorneys do not recommend that anyone engage in business as a sole proprietor.

Chapter **4**

An Overview of Partnerships

P artnerships are divided into several subcategories. The first and most basic is the general partnership. A general partnership is created when two or more people start a business to produce a profit. It is the default entity (much like a sole proprietorship is for a single owner) when you begin to work with a partner, and do not formalize the business as a specific entity. A general partnership is similar to a sole proprietorship in that there are no asset protection advantages to having a partnership. In other words, if the partnership gets sued, the owners of the company also get sued. Likewise, the law considers that each partner acts at the behest of all partners. Therefore, all owners personally hire all employees, making them personally liable for the acts of each of those employees. It can be worse if your business venture fails and is unable to pay its creditors. In that situation, all of the creditors for that business could come after you, individually, for all of the company's debt. Based on the aforementioned, we would not advise that anyone engage in a general partnership in order to do business.

The general partnership is not without benefits. They are they are easy to create and require no formal document preparation. Taxation is also relatively straight forward, as any profits or write-offs are passed directly to the owners.

Limited partnerships are different. A limited partnership also requires two or more owners; however, only one partner is designated as a general partner- the remaining are listed as limited partners. The general partner has unlimited personal liability in all of the same ways as stated above. Limited partners, however, have some liability protection. Unfortunately, as limited partners they cannot participate in the management of the business, making their role as a partner passive.

The limited liability partnership (LLP) is the most current version of the partnership model. It emerged early in the 1990s as an alternative to the liability issues identified in limited partnerships and general partnerships. In 1992, only two states recognized the LLP entity, but now, over forty states have adopted legislation recognizing the LLP. The tremendous benefit of the LLP is that it limits liability to all partners. In that respect, it has similarities to the limited liability company and the corporation. Unlike the limited partnership, the LLP partners have the right to manage the business directly.

The LLP is a popular form of organization for professionals like lawyers, accountants, and architects. In fact, California, New York, Oregon, and Nevada, reserve LLP formation to only professionals. However, in many other states, it is used by individuals wanting to be taxed as partners with the benefits of limited liability. The formation of the LLP is usually accomplished by filing documentation with your state's secretary of state's office or with the department of commerce.

Similar to the Uniform Probate Code we discussed above, there is also a Uniform Partnership Act (UPA). The UPA has been around for over a century and is a general guideline to consider. Because there have been extensive revisions to the UPA over the years, many practitioners refer to the Revised Uniform Partnership Act (RUPA) when speaking of more current versions. We will not be so precise and will simply refer to it as the UPA. However, we will reference the most recent and updated version available. At least some version of the UPA has been adopted by thirty-eight states, making it worthy of consideration as a general overview.

When considering a partnership arrangement, you must consider the liabilities that partnership creates in order to assess the impact of a partnership on your asset protection plan and strategy. Consider some of the language of the Act:

Uniform Partnership Act (1997)

Section 202 — Formation of Partnership

(a) Except as otherwise provided in subsection (b), the association of two or more persons to carry on as co-owners a business for profit forms a partnership, whether or not the persons intend to form a partnership.

(b) An association formed under a statute other than this [Act], a predecessor statute, or a comparable statute of another jurisdiction is not a partnership under this [Act].

(c) In determining whether a partnership is formed, the following rules apply:

(1) Joint tenancy, tenancy in common, tenancy by the entireties, joint property, common property, or part ownership does not by itself establish a partnership, even if the co-owners share profits made by the use of the property.

(2) The sharing of gross returns does not by itself establish a partnership, even if the persons sharing them have a joint or common right or interest in property from which the returns are derived.

(3) A person who receives a share of the profits of a business is presumed to be a
partner in the business, unless the profits were received in payment:

(i) of a debt by installments or otherwise;

(ii) for services as an independent contractor or of wages or other compensation to an employee;

(iii) of rent;

(iv) of an annuity or other retirement or health benefit to a beneficiary, representative, or designee of a deceased or retired partner;

(v) of interest or other charge on a loan, even if the amount of payment varies with the profits of the business, including a direct or indirect present or future ownership of the collateral, or rights to income, proceeds, or increase in value derived from the collateral; or

(vi) for the sale of the goodwill of a business or other property by installments or otherwise.

Section 203 — Partnership Property

Property acquired by a partnership is property of the partnership and not of the partners individually.

Section 204 — When Property is Partnership Property

(a) Property is partnership property if acquired in the name of:

(1) the partnership; or
(2) one or more partners with an indication in the instrument transferring title to the property of the person's capacity as a partner or of the existence of a partnership but without an indication of the name of the partnership.

(b) Property is acquired in the name of the partnership by a transfer to:

(1) the partnership in its name; or
(2) one or more partners in their capacity as partners in the partnership, if the name of the partnership is indicated in the instrument transferring title to the property.

(c) Property is presumed to be partnership property if purchased with partnership assets, even if not acquired in the name of the partnership or of one or more partners with an indication in the instrument transferring title to the property of the person's capacity as a partner or of the existence of a partnership.

(d) Property acquired in the name of one or more of the partners, without an indication in the instrument transferring title to the property of the person's capacity as a partner or of the existence of a partnership and without use of partnership assets, is presumed to be separate property, even if used for partnership purposes.

Section 301 — Partner Agent of Partnership

Subject to the effect of a statement of partnership authority under Section 303:

(1) Each partner is an agent of the partnership for the purpose of its business. An act of a partner, including the execution of an instrument in the partnership name, for apparently carrying on in the ordinary course the partnership business or business of the kind carried on by the partnership binds the partnership, unless the partner had no authority to act for the partnership in the particular matter and the person with whom the partner was dealing knew or had received a notification that the partner lacked authority.

(2) An act of a partner which is not apparently for carrying on in the ordinary course the partnership business or business of the kind carried on by the partnership binds the partnership only if the act was authorized by the other partners.

Those interested in looking at other provisions of the UPA should be able to find it easily online. Many law libraries provide free access to it and any popular search engine will direct you [6].

---

[6] Two great online resources include the Law Library of Cornell, found at www.law.cornell. edu and the Law Library of the University of Pennsylvania, found at www.upenn.edu.

Family Limited Partnerships

A family limited partnership (FLP) is a very powerful estate planning and asset protection tool. If utilized correctly, an individual can cut their estate taxes, and by spreading income among members of their family who reside in lower tax brackets, they can also lower their overall income tax rates. FLPs are so effective, in fact, that up until a few years ago, the IRS was adamant about them being a form of tax dodging rather than a real, and legal, tax strategy.

An FLP is a limited partnership that holds the family business or investments. The whole idea is based on the belief that the parents will make a gift of their interests in the limited partnership to their children.

Limited partnerships are not "liquid," meaning that the discounts received from the government would be quite substantial. But only if you don't make the same mistakes that so many others do when setting up their family limited partnerships.

One of the most common mistakes people make when setting up their FLP is that they usually fail to maintain it once it gets off the ground. Annual fees are required to keep an FLP afloat, and when you stop making these payments your family limited partnership goes into default and its registration expires. When this happens, you kill the FLP, and it ceases to exist in the eyes of the state and the IRS.

Another monumental mistake when using an FLP is making a parent the general partner. The charging order, which is discussed in depth later on in this book, only applies if the general partner does NOT make distributions into the interests held by the limited partner for the overall benefit of a creditor.

If it is a mistake to have the parent as a general partner, then it is an even bigger one to have the parent as both the general and limited partner. When the parent takes the position of both general and limited partner, they run the risk of having a court declare there is no partnership at all since the parent maintains ownership of the entire FLP interests.

As you can see, individuals may make numerous mistakes when dealing with an FLP, such as those discussed above, or by using the FLP to pay for personal or household expenses. To succeed using an FLP, much detail and understanding of the protocols surrounding FLPs is required. As is our theme throughout the book, sometimes it is better to consult a competent professional than to attempt to set up an FLP by yourself. FLPs are useful enough to the everyday man that any misstep could be used as grounds by the government to have it disregarded.

With an FLP, your children and grandchildren can help in the growth of the assets. Not only are their tax rates lower than yours are, but if the FLP happens to be helping pay for their education and certain other needs, then the FLP automatically gets a net reduction of the cost provided for such things. Any family members who provide certain services for the business can be paid for their services.

Also, as the general partner, should your family require a loan of some sort for a specific need, like education or starting up a business, you have the ability to make that happen as long as there is an agreement for the money to be repaid at a later date. In the event that both parents are general partners and one becomes disabled or dies, then the spouse will then be fully equipped to carry on the running of the partnership.

An FLP maintains the privacy of a partnership from the public record, leaves the company itself organized in the event that a parent passes away, and allows the family (specifically the children, or other intended successors) to work closely in the running of the business. It is also a very effective building block for investments. As evidenced above, what a family limited partnership has to offer is limitless; you just have to know how to take advantage of it.

How Can You Maintain Control and Pass Ownership to Children?

All the talk of FLPs brings us to our next topic. Imagine that you have children to whom you wished to pass your business. If your children are too young, unprepared for the responsibilities of the business, or if you have simply reached a beneficial agreement as to the terms of your working relationship, how exactly do you think you would go about passing ownership over to them without giving up control of the business?

While it is possible to gift the business to your family while you're still living, the amount of time it would take and the fact that you give up control, make this an impractical solution. The exception is if you have long-term plans, such as making annual gifts (no more than $12,000 of which can be sent without a tax per person) either directly to your children or grandchildren, or in a trust fund. The best thing about this solution is that you can make the gift as large as you want, if you don't mind the added tax, so that you won't have to inform the IRS.

Any competent individual is able to act as a general partner in a limited partnership, a child, a limited liability company, a business associate, a trust, and even a corporation. When the parent is a general partner, they have the ability to convey only the interest of a limited partner, but in such a way that they are not moving the asset itself. By doing this, the parent stays in control of the business while slowly handing over ownership of the company.

Chapter **5**

An Overview of Corporations

A corporation is a legal entity that exists only in the contemplation of law, which is separate and distinct from its owners, who are also known as shareholders. This means that we create a legal person on paper. This legal person is called a corporation. Under the law, a corporation is considered and treated as a separate person for legal and tax purposes so long as corporate formalities are followed.

A corporation can be a good asset protection vehicle because it can shield an individual's personal assets from the business's assets and liabilities. This corporate shield is also known as the corporate veil. In order to maintain this corporate shield and protection for the shareholders and the officers of the corporation, there are corporate formalities which must be followed.

These formalities include the adoption of a set of bylaws, which provide a written statement of how the internal affairs of the corporation will be handled. The bylaws set the time and place of regular shareholder meetings and meetings of the board of directors.

The corporation must also maintain a minute book. A corporate minute book contains a written record of the actions by the shareholders and directors of the corporation. At a minimum, there must be annual minutes reflecting the election of directors by the shareholders. Any significant corporate activities, including corporate borrowing, purchases, and the payment of compensation to officers, should be properly reflected in the minutes of the meetings of directors and shareholders.

The corporation must maintain an accurate stock ledger book. This ledger book shows to whom stock certificates have been issued and the amounts received by the corporation for the issuance of its stock. The stock ledger book contains an up-to-date record of the number of shares owned by each shareholder, as well as each shareholder's name.

When doing business with third parties, the officers and directors must make it clear that they are acting on behalf of the corporation and not in their individual capacity. Correspondence should be sent out under the proper corporate letterhead, and contracts should be entered into only with the corporation as a signatory. Unless the documents clearly reflect that the transaction is entered into on behalf of the corporation and all necessary agreements are entered into under the corporation's name, the corporate entity will not survive a challenge in a lawsuit.

Corporate bank accounts and accounting records must be separate and distinct from the individual. A corporate bank account cannot be treated as if it were the account of an individual officer or director. The corporate veil hinges upon the legal fiction that a corporation is a separate legal entity apart from its owners, officers, and directors. To maintain this legal entity, you must treat the corporation as a separate entity. This means you must keep all financial books and financial records for the corporation completely separate. You must not use corporate funds to pay for personal debt. Co-mingling funds is one of the worst things you can do in corporate accounting. Corporate income and assets must be separately accounted for in the books of the corporation. One of the biggest mistakes made by individuals is that they feel they can freely move money back and forth between themselves and their corporation without properly accounting for the movement in the records of the corporation. This is a fatal mistake, and under these circumstances, the corporate entity may be disregarded by a court of law if challenged.

Case law on the corporation is robust and in whatever jurisdiction you reside, you will find differences in how corporations are viewed and considered by each state. But there are some general concepts that apply to each, regardless of the jurisdiction where you reside.

The first is known as the duty of care. The duty of care states that directors and officers of a corporation are required by law to perform their obligations in those capacities in accordance with a minimum standard of care. Courts apply the duty of care in cases involving alleged negligence, mismanagement, or intentional decisions to commit unlawful acts. The standard of care for directors and officers of business corporations is derived from common law and state business corporation codes. This standard is often tempered by the business judgment rule. Under the business judgment rule, a court will generally refuse to second-guess a business decision, so long as management made a reasonable effort to make an informed decision. The bottom line for those considering a corporation as an asset protection tool is that you must remember that by

using a corporation, new duties and obligations arise that may require active participation on your part.

Next, directors and officers have a fiduciary relationship to the corporation and its shareholders. Because corporate directors and officers occupy a fiduciary capacity, they must exercise the utmost good faith in all transactions in regards to their duties to the corporation and its property. What this means is, that in their dealings with and for the corporation they are held to the same strict rule of honesty and fair dealing between themselves and their principle as other agents.

The fiduciary duty runs to shareholders and the corporation, but not necessarily to fellow officers or directors except to the extent they are shareholders. The fiduciary duty attaching to an officer or director is inherent in the office and does not require a showing that the officer or director occupied a position of trust or had superior knowledge. Persons who hold positions simultaneously as officers and directors of a corporation may be held to even higher standards than the normal and demanding standards that apply to fiduciaries.

In other words, a director or officer of a corporation owes the corporation complete loyalty, honesty, and good faith. That duty is owed the corporation and its shareholders whenever the actions of the director or officer concern matters affecting the general well-being of the corporation. Thus, as a fiduciary in this sense, a director's or officer's first duty is to act in all things of trust wholly for the benefit of the corporation. This encompasses a duty to disclose information to those who have a right to know the facts.

The rule applies equally to persons purporting to act as directors or officers of a corporation, and they are liable if they act in bad faith whether they are directors de jure or de facto. As agents entrusted with the management of the corporation for the benefit of the shareholders collectively, they occupy a fiduciary relation, and in this sense, the relation is one of trust. Accordingly, a director or officer may not secure a private advantage at the expense of the corporation, and a duty is owed to the corporation and shareholders to make a full and frank disclosure of all the circumstances when seeking ratification of a course of conduct.

Directors or officers must act in the utmost good faith, and this good faith forbids placing themselves in a position where their individual interest clashes with their duty to the corporation. If a director, or officer, places him or herself in a position in which the director or officer may be tempted by his or her own private interest, to disregard that of the corporation, the transactions are voidable at the option of the corporation and may be set aside without a showing of actual injury. When bad faith motivates an act otherwise within a director's or officer's authority, a cause of action based upon a breach of fiduciary duty results.

Before proceeding to show that an individual breached a fiduciary duty owed to the corporation, it must first be established that the defendant is an officer of the corporation who would owe such a duty. A corporate officer owing fiduciary duty to the corporation is a person charged with important functions of management, such as president, vice-president, or treasurer. Nominal corporate officers, with no management authority, are not fiduciaries of the corporation.

Among the factors a court may consider in determining whether an employee is an officer owing fiduciary duties to the corporation are the employee's managerial duties, whether the position occupied is one of authority, and whether the employee possesses superior knowledge and influence over another and is in a position of trust. There is no distinction in the degree of fiduciary obligation that may be recognized based upon the degree of corporate involvement of an officer or director. It is the nature of the position itself, and not the nature of the specific responsibilities that may be assumed, that give rise to the obligation.

While it is the general rule that a plaintiff carries the burden of proof on a complaint, where a violation of fiduciary duty is involved, the fiduciary must establish that his or her obligations were properly discharged. However, once a fiduciary's self-dealing or personal benefit in one transaction has been shown, the burden does not shift to the fiduciary to prove the fairness of all transactions complained of, regardless of whether any evidence has been presented that such transactions involved self-dealing or personal benefit. In a shareholder derivative action, the plaintiff bears the burden of proving a breach of fiduciary duty to the corporation and that the breach was the proximate cause of the losses sustained.

A director or officer may be liable for a violation of fiduciary duty even in the absence of bad faith or dishonesty; affirmative malfeasance is not required—mere passive negligence can be enough to breach the duty and result in liability. Similarly, a director or officer who fails to take the necessary steps to acquire a rudimentary understanding of the business and activities of the corporation may be held liable for damage resulting from that ignorance. Generally, any alleged breach of a fiduciary duty is a question for the trier of fact after examination of all the evidence.

Directors and officers cannot manipulate the affairs of the corporation primarily with the design of securing the control of the corporation to one particular group of shareholders, or of excluding another group from the exercise of its corporate rights. A director or officer's fiduciary duty is to the corporation, not to his or her fellow officers or directors.

Directors and officers may not unlawfully divert the proceeds of the corporation's capital or other assets but must exercise their authority with the utmost good faith. The individual directors or officers of one corporation cannot lawfully take the funds of the corporation, and turn them over to another corporation, unless their action is authorized by their corporationin some proper way. The directors and officers may be compelled to account to the corporation for sums of money received by them as bonus payments to which they were not entitled.

However, the fiduciary relationship does not make an officer liable as an insurer. A director is not an insurer and, therefore, a director is not liable for a loss of corporate assets unless the director was negligent, and if negligent, the negligence was the cause of the loss.

Rights of action against officers, directors and shareholders of a corporation for breaches of fiduciary duties, which can be enforced by either the corporation directly, or the shareholders derivatively, before bankruptcy, become the property of the estate, which the trustee alone has the right to pursue after the filing of a bankruptcy petition.

The fiduciary obligations of a close corporation's directors or officers are not relaxed any more than in other corporations. Close corporation shareholders as such, stand in a fiduciary relationship to each other. It has been said that the shareholders and directors of a close corporation are subject to a particularly rigorous fiduciary standard, comparable to that of partners or joint venturers. Furthermore, shareholders of a closely held corporation cannot escape liability by failing to observe the formality of electing directors when they exercise all powers and undertake all activities of directors. Thus, where the relevant business closely resembles a family business or complex family partnership doing business through numerous entities of varied legal forms, the corporate directors' fiduciary duties may include furthering the interests of each other, rather than merely furthering the interests of the business enterprise.

In close corporations, all shareholders should be treated fairly, and their investments protected because minority shareholders may easily be reduced to insignificance and their investment rendered captive. In a small, closely-held corporation, the officers and directors' duty to the corporation may also be reciprocal between the officers and directors of the corporation.

Confidential information acquired or compiled by a corporation in the course and conduct of its business is a species of property to which the corporation has the exclusive right and benefit, and which a court of equity will protect through the injunctive process or other appropriate remedy. In determining whether information is confidential, the following factors are relevant: (1) the protected matter is not generally known or readily ascertainable; (2) it provides a demonstrable competitive advantage; (3) it was gained at expense to the employer; and (4) it is such that the employer intended to keep it confidential.

Thus, where an officer, director, employee, or shareholder of the corporation who acquires or is given access to such information in confidence, who adopts and uses it for his or her own private benefit and personal profit, to the exclusion and detriment of the corporation-he or she may be enjoined at the insistence of the corporation, and he or she may be required to account to the corporation for any profits derived from the information, as well as be subject to liability for damages sustained by the corporation as a result of such breach of fiduciary duties. A corporation that is not actually deprived of its confidential business information may still suffer injury if it is denied the right to exclusive use of its confidential information.

The corporation may obtain injunctive or other appropriate relief against the abuse or misuse of such information by a former officer or employee, or a third person. The rule is limited, however, by the principle that a former employee is free to make use of the information, skill, and knowledge acquired while associated with the former employer; only trade secrets or confidential information and corporate property are proscribed from use in a competing business. Even where the corporate property appropriated is a trade secret, generally the corporation is not entitled to a permanent injunction against its use, but only to a temporary injunction for the period of time it would have taken the former employee to secure the information by independent means. Likewise, in a suit for damages, the market value of the appropriated property is determined only with respect to this limited period before the former employee could have obtained the same information from other sources.

A corporate fiduciary entrusted with valuable or potentially valuable corporate information may not appropriate that asset for his or her own use, even though in so doing, the fiduciary causes no injury to the corporation. In other words, officers and directors cannot retain for themselves profits that they have derived solely from exploiting information gained by virtue of their inside position as corporate officials.

These principles have been applied in cases involving trade secrets, lists of customers, accounts and insurance policyholders, as well as in cases pertaining to confidential or inside financial or other material information relative to the corporation, such as in connection with transactions involving corporate stock or other securities.

The "S" and "C" Corporation

When "C" corporation is used in this book, it refers to a corporation that has chosen a designation within the Internal Revenue Service regarding how that entity is taxed. Likewise, when "S" corporation is used in this book, it refers to a corporation that has chosen a designation within the Internal Revenue Service regarding how that entity is taxed. As you might suspect, a C corporation and an S corporation are taxed differently. A C corporation is taxed separately and all income received by the shareholders is also taxed. This means that the owners of a C corporation are effectively taxed twice: once at the corporate level and once at the personal level. An S corporation allows the owners to be taxed only once - at the personal level for that corporation. Election for an S corporation is done by completing Form 2553 with the Internal Revenue Service. Several requirements must be met in order to meet the S corporation election. For example, an entity such as an LLC or trust cannot be a shareholder of an S corporation. Most small businesses choose to be taxed as an S Corporation because of the great tax benefits that are forwarded to the owners. The shareholders are not taxed on dividends and do not have to pay a self-employment tax when operating a business out of an S corporation. Additionally, the S corporation can offer some great asset protection strategies, and is a tool that can definitely be used depending on the business that is being operated.

Dissolution of a Corporation

In the United States, the statistics of a business succeeding are dismal. Currently nine out of ten businesses started in the United States go out of business within one year. Of the ones that survive, nine out of ten fail within the next five years. Therefore, it seems prudent to include some instruction as to how to end or dissolve a business. There are essentially six steps involved in dissolving a corporation, whether it's a limited liability company or nonprofit corporation.

First, the corporation must hold a meeting. Usually, this is a special meeting of shareholders which must be properly noticed by the board of directors. The notice of the special meeting must specifically outline that it will transact the business by considering a plan to liquidate the company, distribute the assets to the shareholders, dissolve the company, and approve the articles of dissolution for filing with the Secretary of State and Department of Commerce. After the meeting is held and approved, articles of dissolution should be properly generated and filed with the proper state, federal, and government authorities as needed. Then, in the event of dissolution, a statutory notification should be sent to creditors. The notice to creditors should outline that the corporation has been dissolved or has filed the statement of intent to dissolve with the proper government authority. It should state the mailing address where creditors should send their claims, should they have any. It must also provide a list of information to be included with the claim, such as the account number, consideration for the debt, the date the debt was incurred, and the amount of the obligation owed. The deadline for submitting claims is usually 120 days after the date of the notice, and a statement should be made that the claims will be barred if not received by the deadline.

After the expiration of the 120 days, the corporation should settle all creditor claims and then distribute any remaining business assets to the shareholders or liquidate them and provide liquid assets to the shareholders pursuant to their ownership in the business.

Personal Liability in Corporations

An individual is personally liable for all torts which that individual committed, even though the person may have acted as an agent or under the directions of another. This rule applies to torts committed by those acting in their official capacities as officers or agents of a corporation. It is immaterial that the corporation may also be liable. Under the responsible corporate officer doctrine, if a corporate officer participates in wrongful conduct, or knowingly approves the conduct, the officer, as well as the corporation, is liable for the penalties. The responsible corporate officer doctrine applies to public welfare offenses that impose strict liability by plain language and intent. The person injured may hold either liable, and generally the injured person may hold both as a joint tortfeasors.

Corporate officers are liable for their torts, although committed when acting officially, even though the acts were performed for the benefit of the corporation and without profit to the officer personally. Corporate officers charged in law with affirmative official responsibility in the management and control of the corporate business, cannot avoid personal liability for wrongs committed by claiming that they did not authorize and direct that which was done in the regular course of that business, with their knowledge and with their consent or approval, or such acquiescence on their part as warrants inferring such consent or approval. However, more than mere knowledge may be required in order to hold an officer liable. The plaintiff must show some form of participation by the officer in the tort, or at least show that the officer directed, controlled, approved, or ratified the decision which led to the plaintiff's injury.

If an officer or director has constructive knowledge of fraudulent acts, it may be enough to attach personal liability. Circumstantial evidence, such as the way a corporation transacts business, can be used to prove constructive knowledge and direct evidence may not be needed. A corporate officer or director may not seek shelter from liability in the defense that he or she was only following orders. Personal liability attaches, regardless of whether the breach was accomplished through malfeasance, misfeasance, or nonfeasance. However, there is authority that a corporate officer cannot be held personally liable for nonfeasance.

Personal liability for the torts of officers does not depend on the same grounds as "piercing the corporate veil," that is inadequate capitalization, use of the corporate form for fraudulent purposes, or failure to comply with the formalities of corporate organization. The true basis of liability is the officer's violation of some duty owed to the third person, which injures the third person.

Corporate shareholders generally are shielded from personal liability for corporate debts and liabilities. The prevailing rule is that when corporate formalities are observed, initial corporate financing is adequate, and the corporation is not formed or availed to cheat or defraud creditors and other third parties, the corporate form is respected and shareholders are not liable for corporate debts and liabilities.

Although the liability protection provided by using the corporate form, under common law equitable principles, the corporate entity may be disregarded, and the shareholders subjected to personal liability when the concept of a separate legal entity defeats public policy or protects fraudulent acts. A good example of how courts consider the corporation status can be found in the case U.S. v. Milwaukee Refrigerator Transit Co. Judge Sanborn stated:

> [A] corporation will be looked upon as a legal entity, as a general rule, and until sufficient reason to the contrary appears; but, when the notion of legal entity is used to defeat public convenience, justify wrong, protect fraud, or defend crime, the law will regard the corporation as an association of persons ....

The piercing the corporate veil issue is one of the most frequently litigated issues in corporate law. The courts generally have conditioned recognition of the corporate entity for liability purposes on compliance, with the requirement that business be conducted on a corporate, rather than a personal, basis, and that the business enterprise be created with adequate financial means. For example, Ramsey v. Adams, lists eight significant factors for piercing the corporate veil:

(1) undercapitalization;

(2) nonobservance of corporate formalities (e.g., failure to hold director and shareholder meetings, failure to maintain minutes, failure to maintain corporate records);

(3) nonpayment of dividends;

(4) siphoning of funds by controlling shareholders for their personal use;

(5) nonfunctioning officers and directors;

(6) absence of corporate records;

(7) use of the corporate entity as facade for the personal operations of the controlling shareholder; and,

(8) use of the corporate entity to promote fraud or injustice.

When a court decides that the corporate entity should not be respected, only those shareholders who cause the piercing are personally liable for the corporation's debts and liabilities. Passive shareholders have little risk.

The Model Business Corporation Act

The Model Business Corporation Act (MBCA) is a model set of laws prepared by a committee. It has been adopted by twenty-four states in some fashion. The MBCA has been updated several times over the years, and the revised version is sometimes referred to as the Revised Model Business Corporation Act (RMBCA). We will simply refer to it as the MBCA. The MBCA is a well-developed document, spanning nearly one thousand pages. Therefore, we can only make mention of some highlights [7].

MODEL BUSINESS CORPORATION ACT (2005)

Section 2.01 — Incorporators

One or more persons may act as the incorporator or incorporators of a corporation by delivering articles of incorporation to the secretary of state for filing.

Section 2.02 — Articles of Incorporation

(a) The articles of incorporation must set forth:
  (1) A corporate name for the corporation that satisfies the requirements of section 4.01
  (2) The number of shares the corporation is authorized to issue

---

[7]For more information about the Model Business Corporation Act you may visit the American Bar Association at www.americanbar.org.

(3) The street address of the corporation's initial registered office and the name of its initial registered agent at that office

(4) The name and address of each incorporator.

(b) The articles of incorporation may set forth:

(1) The names and addresses of the individuals who are to serve as the initial directors;

(2) Provisions not inconsistent with law regarding:
  (i)   The purpose or purposes for which the corporation is organized
  (ii) Managing the business and regulating the affairs of the corporation
  (iii) Defining, limiting, and regulating the powers of the corporation, its board of directors, and shareholders
  (iv) A par value for authorized shares or classes of shares
  (v)   The imposition of personal liability on shareholders for the debts of the corporation to a specified extent and upon specified conditions

(3) Any provision that under this Act is required or permitted to be set forth in the bylaws

(4) A provision eliminating or limiting the liability of a director to the corporation or its shareholders for money damages for any action taken, or any failure to take any action, as a director, except liability for (A) the amount of a financial benefit received by a director to which he is not entitled; (B) an intentional infliction of harm on the corporation or the shareholders; (C) a violation of section 8.33; or (D) an intentional violation of criminal law

(5) A provision permitting or making obligatory indemnification of a director for liability (as defined in section 8.50(5)) to any person for any action taken, or any failure to take any action, as a director, except liability for (A) receipt of a financial benefit to which he is not entitled, (B) an intentional infliction of harm on the corporation or its shareholders, (C) a violation of section 8.33, or (D) an intentional violation of criminal law.

(c) The articles of incorporation need not set forth any of the corporate powers enumerated in this Act.

(d) Provisions of the articles of incorporation may be made dependent upon facts objectively ascertainable outside the articles of incorporation in accordance with section 1.20(k).

Section 2.03 — Incorporation

(a) Unless a delayed effective date is specified, the corporate existence begins when the articles of incorporation are filed.

(b) The secretary of state's filing of the articles of incorporation is conclusive proof that the incorporators satisfied all conditions precedent to incorporation except in a proceeding by the state to cancel or revoke the incorporation or involuntarily dissolve the corporation

Section 2.04 — Liability for Preincorporation Transactions

All persons purporting to act as or on behalf of a corporation, knowing there was no incorporation under this Act, are jointly and severally liable for all liabilities created while so acting.

Section 2.05 — Organization of Corporation

(a) After incorporation:

(1) If initial directors are named in the articles of incorporation, the initial directors shall hold an organizational meeting, at the call of a majority of the directors, to complete the organization of the corporation by appointing officers, adopting bylaws, and carrying on any other business brought before the meeting;

(2) If initial directors are not named in the articles, the incorporator or incorporators shall hold an organizational meeting at the call of a majority of the incorporators:

(i) to elect directors and complete the organization of the corporation; or

(ii) to elect a board of directors who shall complete the organization of the corporation.

(b) Action required or permitted by this Act to be taken by incorporators at an organizational meeting may be taken without a meeting if the action taken is evidenced by one or more written consents describing the action taken and signed by each incorporator.

(c) An organizational meeting may be held in or out of this state.

Section 2.06 — Bylaws

(a) The incorporators or board of directors of a corporation shall adopt initial bylaws for the corporation.

(b) The bylaws of a corporation may contain any provision for managing the business and regulating the affairs of the corporation that is not inconsistent with law or the articles of incorporation.

Utilizing the Strength of a Corporate Structure to Protect Your Assets

The definition of a corporation is a legal entity which is separate and distinct from the person or persons that own it. Corporations have existed in the United States since the birth of the nation, and they even existed prior to that in England, Denmark, and many other countries. In the United States, there are two types of taxable corporations: the C corporation and the S corporation. The distinction between a C corporation and an S corporation is the way each is taxed and how each is treated by the Internal Revenue Service. Most small businesses elect to be treated as an S corporation in order to take advantage of certain tax benefits under subsection S of the Internal Revenue Code. Larger corporations, such as publicly traded corporations, are usually taxed under subsection C of the code.

A corporation is formed by filing articles of incorporation with the appropriate secretary of state or department of commerce where the corporation is to be formed. Usually, articles of incorporation are filed with the department of commerce. For example, when you hear the term, a "Delaware Corporation," it means that the corporation was formed under the laws of the state of Delaware.

A foreign corporation is a corporation that exists outside of the state in which business is taking place. For example, a Delaware corporation as well as a company set up in Panama would both be foreign to the state of California.

Articles of incorporation generally must adhere to certain formalities. They must include the name of the company, name and address of each of the incorporators, and the names and addresses of the individuals who are to serve as the initial directors of the corporation. The Articles must include who must designate a registered agent and the address of that agent, along with an acknowledgement that the agent accepts the duties of a registered agent.

The articles must also contain the purpose and the duration for the corporation, along with the types of shares that the corporation will issue; whether those shares are voting or nonvoting; and whether any dividends will be issued by the same. In most states, the articles of incorporation must be typed in English.

After the articles of incorporation have been filed, date stamped, and approved, the corporation needs to hold its first meeting of shareholders, elect officers for the corporation, and finally enact bylaws.

Some people may be confused as to how a corporation operates, how liable the corporation might be, as well as to how liable the shareholders might be for acts performed by a corporation. Essentially, the shareholders elect directors and the directors of the corporation appoint officers. The officers conduct and manage the affairs and operations of the corporation. Since the corporation is a separate legal entity from the individuals owning the shares, shareholders are usually not liable for acts of a corporation. Shareholders can only be found legally responsible for the acts of a corporation if a creditor in a lawsuit is able to 'pierce the corporate veil.'

How does a creditor pierce the corporate veil? The easiest way a creditor can sue a corporation and pierce the corporate veil to access the assets of the individual shareholders is by showing that the corporation did not abide by corporate formalities. Corporate formalities include:

1) Signing the articles of incorporation
2) Adopting a set of bylaws in the corporate records
3) Setting up a distinct bank account for the corporation
4) Conducting annual meetings of shareholders
5) Maintaining an arm's length transaction between the shareholders and the corporation
6) Paying dividends as required
7) Maintaining functioning officers and directors for the corporation
8) Maintaining proper capitalization of the corporation and

any other facts that a court may deem relevant

Essentially, shareholders of a corporation must maintain the corporate entity as a separate and distinct entity. A single individual can form and establish a corporation. However, if that individual combines his or her own funds with the corporation's bank account and uses the corporation to pay for his or her personal expenses, the corporation is basically being used as a façade and is, therefore, a sham. Anytime an individual uses the assets of a corporation as his or her own, a court may determine that the individual was simply acting as the corporation and that the corporate entity should be set aside or that the corporate veil should be pierced.

The way to avoid liability when conducting business in a corporation or other legal entity is to follow all corporate formalities and not engage in any fraud. Here is an example of where a corporation may be exposed to the alter ego theory of piercing the corporate veil.

Let us use an example of John Doe and Jane Doe where John Doe owns a construction company. Let's say that John Doe's construction company was formed as a corporation where he designated (under the Internal Revenue Code) that he would conduct business as an S corporation and that he alone would be the sole shareholder. Perhaps he obtained a form from the Internet or another source and filed the articles of incorporation with the Department of Commerce. Whatever his method, after filing the document, he put his articles of incorporation in a file folder in his desk drawer at home.

John Doe then began operating his business —John Doe's Construction Company—, and whenever he received checks for the construction company, he would then put those checks in his personal account. He never opened up a bank account for his construction company, he never held a meeting for the shareholders, and he never issued the stock that he said he would issue in his articles of incorporation. Taking a look at John Doe's checkbook, you would note that expenses for groceries, his cable bill, his car payment, his house payment and all of his supplies and business expenses were all taken from his personal checkbook.

This example demonstrates how John Doe failed to keep the corporate formalities. It's obvious at this point that John Doe should have issued stock certificates to himself if he was the sole owner, at least held annual meetings of shareholders to elect himself as a director, appointed himself as an officer of the company, opened up a separate bank account, and completed the IRS SS-4 form (this gives him an Employer Identification Number (EIN) with the Internal Revenue Service (IRS)). Then, he could have submitted Form 2553 to the IRS within the appropriate time frame to be designated an S Corporation.

By failing to do these things, John Doe has exposed himself to liability for all of the corporation's actions and debts. If such evidence were presented to a judge in a court of law, the court could, under these circumstances, pierce the corporate veil and access all of John Doe's personal assets for acts done by the corporation.

Keeping your money separate from the corporation's money is an essential step that should be taken care of if you wish to maintain the corporate veil. You can also maintain the corporate veil by keeping a corporate minute book and other corporate records, issuing bylaws and abiding by them, issuing stock certificates to the shareholders of the corporation, and maintaining separate records for any and all other entities where you are an owner.

When executing legal contracts or agreements, you should execute them on behalf of the company by signing them in the name of the corporation. Sign your name as the officer and in whatever office you hold in relation to that company. Any major action for the corporation should be brought before the board of directors, and the officers should obtain approval for that major action. Any meeting should be recorded and placed in the company record book. Doing these things will minimize your liability and exposure to lawsuits. These actions will also prevent possible bankruptcy trustees from taking corporation assets and claiming that they are yours.

Limited Liability

A liability is where one is legally obligated and responsible for something. For example, if you go into a store, purchase groceries, and use your credit card, you are liable or legally responsible to the credit card company who issued that credit card to you (per your credit card agreement) to repay the amount that you spent at the grocery store. A limitation on liability, or having limited liability, means that your exposure to risk has been limited or reduced. Many asset protection attorneys advise clients to have a corporation properly in place to limit the owner's or shareholder's liability. This is a valid strategy if done correctly.

In a lawsuit situation, if a creditor files a lawsuit against you to recover funds owed to them, and you are the shareholder of the corporation and have properly maintained the corporate entity, you are not individually responsible for any debt that is owed by that corporation to the creditor. This limits your liability. This protects your assets.

Anyone who has opened up a new business, starting with their personal assets, is usually asked to sign a personal guarantee when attempting to get a loan from the bank or when leasing property on behalf of the corporation. This is because banks and landlords understand that if the corporation goes out of business without repaying their loan or without paying their rent, the bank and landlord are left without recourse since the shareholders and directors of the corporation are not usually liable for the debts and liabilities of the corporation.

To avoid being left 'holding the bag,' banks, landlords, and others who extend credit to newly formed corporations, usually require that those who control the corporation sign a personal guarantee. A personal guarantee[8] essentially states if the corporation does not meet its obligations, the signor is required to pay the debt.

---

[8]A personal guarantee is a pledge by a person to a lender to repay a debt on behalf of the corporation or entity if the corporation or entity fails to make the repayment pursuant to the terms of the debt instrument.

There are essentially two types of personal guarantees: sole guarantees and continuing guarantees. A sole personal guarantee will guarantee one act or one debt that is owed by the corporation. Consequently, the person signing the guarantee's liability is limited to that one transaction. On the other hand, a continuing guarantee is one where the individual assumes liability for any past, present, and future obligations that are now owed, were owed, or may be owed in the future by the corporation to the lender or creditor. A continuing guarantee is very similar in nature to a revolving line of credit.

Usually small businesses or newly formed businesses require the shareholders or directors sign personal guarantees, and even continuing guarantees, depending on the type of loan or credit that is sought. It is often recommended that shareholders or directors do not sign such personal guarantees if they can avoid it. This is especially true for continuing guarantees, because if the director or shareholder happens to sell the business or his or her shares later on, those original signers of a continuing guarantee are still liable for any obligations in the future. This could result in them eventually becoming responsible for a debt they knew nothing about and were unprepared for down the road.

It is also common for banks to attempt to cross-collateralize the business assets with the assets owned by the individuals forming or owning the small corporation. Cross collateralization allows the bank to place a lien on your personal or real property that you own. Real property would include your personal residence, any vacation home you might have, or, depending on the cross collateralization clause, a lien against your stocks and/or personal bank accounts.

Cross-collateralization clauses should also be avoided so that if the corporation goes out of business, you do not lose your house, your cars, or any of your personal assets.

Privacy

One advantage of using an attorney in forming your corporation is that the attorney can serve as the registered agent of the corporate entity. This is beneficial in that when a corporate search is done to discover who the registered agent is, your attorney's name will appear instead of your own, and your attorney's address will show up, rather than your home address. This added benefit is also a small form of privacy, because, should the corporation ever get sued, the registered agent is the one who is served by the constable, sheriff, or legal process server; not you or your spouse.

Obviously, there is much to consider when forming a corporation: articles of incorporation, bylaws, corporate minutes, annual meeting notices, and corporate resolutions, just to name a few. It is prudent to obtain competent legal counsel in the formation and maintenance of a corporation to make sure that you are properly protected and that your liability is limited.

Chapter **6**

An Overview of Limited Liability Companies

A limited liability company (LLC) is a non-corporate business entity. Often times you hear individuals call LLCs limited liability corporations. This is not correct. LLCs, as you will see, are by design a substitution to the corporate entity. In an LLC, all members have limited liability protection. Also, all members can participate in management and control of the entity. Finally, if there are two or more members, generally the LLC is taxed as a partnership rather than a corporation for federal income tax purposes. By combining limited personal liability with partnership tax classification, the LLC can provide tremendous advantages that are unavailable to corporations, partnerships, or limited partnerships. Additionally, most states permit single member LLCs, which generally can be entirely disregarded for tax purposes.

LLCs are formed pursuant to various state limited liability company acts and statutes, which generally set forth a series of default rules that direct LLC operation and governance unless the members' operating agreement specifies otherwise. Since they emerged in the 1990s, LLCs have become the most popular form of business entity in the United States. LLCs are often used to create relatively simple business relationships, but they also are used for exceedingly complex, highly structured business organizations.

At times, attorneys will advise individuals to be leery of the LLC because case law is not as developed and as comprehensive as it is for the corporation. We disagree. First, many courts will equally apply corporate concepts to limited liability entities. Second, courts have already considered numerous issues relating to the LLC, including whether LLCs are entities requiring legal counsel to appear in court, whether members' agreements to arbitrate are binding on their LLC in derivative matters, and other procedural litigation matters. In addition, courts have addressed questions of whether attorneys representing LLCs have an attorney-client relationship with individual members. Some courts have held that LLCs resemble limited partnerships and others have held that an LLC should be treated like a corporation.

Clearly, the hallmark of the LLC form is the liability protection statutorily afforded to all members and managers. Limited liability means that owners are not personally liable for the entity's debts and obligations, unless the owner contracts to be personally liable (e.g., owner guarantees of entity debt) or unless the owner is personally negligent.

Limited liability protection makes the LLC similar to the corporation and differentiates it from general and limited partnerships. In general partnerships and limited partnerships, all partners are personally liable for partnership debts and obligations, as stated above, unless the third party transacting business with the partnership agrees not to hold one or more partners personally liable for partnership obligations. Limited partnerships must have at least one general partner who is personally liable for the limited partnership's debts and obligations (unless the firm registers as a limited liability limited partnership).

Because LLC members are protected from the LLC's debts and obligations, the state LLC statutes typically protect creditors by requiring disclosure of members' agreed-upon contributions to the LLC, and by limiting distributions that lawfully can be made to the members so that they do not render the LLC insolvent or unable to pay its debts when due. In this regard, the LLC statutes are more complex than statutes governing general partnerships and limited partnerships.

Most state LLC statutes permit LLC members to participate in LLC management and control without sacrificing their limited liability protection. Conversely, the state LLC statutes permit LLCs to have one or more managers, thereby providing a centralized management option. By permitting member management, LLCs differ from limited partnerships that are unable, or fail to register as limited liability partnerships, which are managed by their general partners, and in which excessive participation causes limited partners to lose their limited liability protection.

The LLC form permits members to obtain personal liability protection without creating a corporate entity. This non-corporate nature creates several important distinctions between LLCs and corporations. First, LLCs are generally not managed by a board of directors or by officers. In most states, management can be decentralized between all members, each of whom is the LLC's agent.
Second, since LLCs are not subject to state corporate laws, many corporate restrictions on finance have been relaxed. For example, in most states, members can promise to make future contributions of money, property, or services to the LLC in exchange for their membership interests. In addition, distributions can be made without creating a surplus account, as with corporations.

Third, LLCs are taxed like partnerships and thereby are able to avoid double taxation. C Corporations are subject to tax at two levels: on corporate earnings, and when distributions are made. LLCs, like partnerships, are not taxed on income at the LLC level. Instead, taxable income and losses flow through the LLC and are taxed at the member level. Members generally are not taxed when distributions are made to them.

Fourth, LLC interests are not freely transferable. The shares of a corporation are generally more readily transferred than the contractual restrictions of an LLC interest. Unlike a shareholder in a corporation, a member in an LLC is able to transfer only his economic interest. He cannot transfer his management interests without the consent of the other managers.

Fifth, unlike corporations, the original LLC statutes were drafted so that LLCs do not have perpetual life and dissolve either at the expiration of some stated term or upon a member's disassociation, unless the other members agree to continue the LLC's business. Thus, the LLC originally was more fragile than the corporation.

Most state LLC statutes have eliminated requirements that the LLC dissolve at the end of a stated term. In addition, the absence of the corporate characteristic of continuity of life is no longer significant in obtaining partnership federal tax classification, and most state LLC statutes have been changed to reduce or eliminate the requirement that a LLC dissolve open member dissociation. Therefore, LLCs generally can be as durable as corporations.

Limitations on Liability Protections Under the Limited Liability Company

As we stated above, the hallmark features of limited liability companies is the members' protection from personal liability for the LLC's debts, obligations, and liabilities. All state LLC statutes expressly state that members are not personally liable for the LLC's debts, liabilities, and obligations. There are a number of exceptions, however, which may make a member liable for the debts of the LLC. First, a member is liable for actions, which directly cause the liability. Persons are always individually liable for their own torts, and if a member, or the agent or employee of a member, commits a tort (e.g., negligence, assault, professional malpractice) in the course of the LLC's business or otherwise, that person is liable for the injury caused. Similarly, a member is liable for contracts he makes on his own behalf, not for the LLC. Also, in some states, omission of the words "limited liability company," or words or initials of similar import might render members personally liable!

Other limitations exist. For example, if a member or manager personally guaranties the LLC's contracts or indemnifies LLC creditors against the LLC's breach of its contracts, the member or manager is personally liable on his or her separate obligation. In the case of smaller, closely held business entities (whether corporations or LLCs), creditors frequently require personal guaranties of entity debts and obligations. The LLC form does not protect members from their separate contracts. Further, some courts have indicated a member's right to indemnification when a member pays a guaranteed obligation where there is a clear nexus between the creditor's guaranty enforcement and the member's participation in the LLC. Finally, Some LLC statutes specifically permit members to create personal liability through provisions in the articles of organization.

Other concerns exist, but they are easily avoided. For example, in some states the LLC statutes state that persons who assume to act as an LLC prior to formation can be liable for all debts and liabilities prior to formation. Thus, members can be liable to third parties if they assume to act for their LLC without setting up the entity or without the authority to do so. No business should be transacted as an LLC until articles of organization are filed with, and accepted by, the appropriate state official.

Next, members of an LLC may be held liable in certain circumstances (e.g., circumstances involving insolvent LLCs) for distributions made to them. For example, a member's liability for his or her contribution obligation and for returned contributions may run both to the LLC and to creditors who extended credit to the LLC in reliance on the member's contribution or contribution obligation. The LLC statutes generally provide that a member's contribution obligation may be waived or compromised with the consent of the other members, but that such waiver or compromise is ineffective with respect to persons who extended credit or whose claim arose before the waiver or compromise. Likewise, if an LLC conveys its assets to the member in fraud of creditors, the creditors may reach the assets on fraudulent conveyance principles. In addition, members can be held personally liable if an LLC's certificate of cancellation is filed before creditor claims are paid or provided for.

Members may also be liable for unpaid employee withholding taxes if they are "responsible" for the LLC's payment of such taxes and as transferees if the LLC distributes assets to them while insolvent and unable to pay its income taxes.

You should also be aware that some state and federal statutes can create particular exceptions to limited liability protection. For example, Rhode Island extends personal liability for failure to maintain workers compensation insurance to LLC managers and members. Similarly, if a member is an "employer" under the Fair Labor Standards Act and state law, the member can be held personally liable for statutory violations.

Finally, but no less importantly is the application of member liability, similar to the common law piercing the corporate veil concept. The veil piercing concept is rarely used by courts, and in our experience, it is a hard standard to reach. But certainly it does occur and sometimes state statutes provide the opportunity. For example, the Colorado LLC Act statutorily applies the "piercing the veil" doctrine, and requires courts to apply Colorado corporate piercing cases to Colorado LLCs. In addition, the Texas LLC Act permits piercing in the case of "actual fraud," and the Illinois LLC Act protects members only to the same extent that shareholders of Illinois corporations are protected in analogous circumstances. The Minnesota LLC Act provides that the case law stating the conditions under which a Minnesota corporation can be pierced also applies to Minnesota LLCs. The West Virginia LLC Act states that members have the same rights and liabilities as shareholders of West Virginia corporations, and implies that the "piercing the veil" concept applies to West Virginia LLCs.

Dissolving a Limited Liability Company

The dissolution and winding-up process is generally the same in each state. The principal state law variations involve whether the LLC is required to file a notice of intent to dissolve, whether the LLC is required to notify its creditors of the impending dissolution, and how the LLC's assets are distributed on dissolution. Variations in the form and contents of the LLC's articles of dissolution also exist and, as with other state law specific questions, it is always necessary to consult the LLC statute in the state of organization. For example, the Tenth Circuit Court of Appeals has interpreted the Oklahoma LLC Act to mandate that an LLC cease to exist as an entity upon the effective date of its articles of dissolution. Therefore, in Oklahoma and in states with similar statutes, the LLC must wind up its affairs before the effective date, which should be carefully chosen to allow sufficient time to wind up. Other statutes presumably will be interpreted to allow a longer winding up period.

Prior to filing articles of dissolution, the LLC should wind up its business, discharge its liabilities or make adequate provisions, and distribute any remaining assets among the members as prescribed by the operating agreement or, in the absence of any provision in the operating agreement, by the LLC statute. After winding up, the LLC should also file articles of dissolution, which must comply with state law. When the articles of dissolution are filed, the LLC ceases to exist.

State LLC statutes generally do not specify the identity, powers, or compensation of the members who participate in the winding up process, and these matters are best addressed in the operating agreement. Some state statutes provide, for example, that the "remaining" members participate in the winding up process, or that members or managers who wrongfully withdraw from the LLC do not participate in the winding up process. In the absence of any provision in the statute or the operating agreement, the LLC likely can be wound up by the members or managers who participated in the LLC's business before dissolution. During winding up, the managers' or members' actual authority to bind the LLC to third parties and to undertake LLC business should be modified to reflect the effect of the dissolution on the LLC's business.

Members and managers may have greater apparent authority to bind the LLC to third parties than they have actual authority, and partnership law should be reviewed in this regard. Members and managers may have continuing apparent authority to bind the LLC to persons who have dealt with the LLC in the past and who do not have knowledge or notice of the dissolution. In addition, the LLC may be bound by acts if the creditor has knowledge of the dissolution, but does not know of the member's or manager's lack of actual authority. Members' and managers' fiduciary duties to the LLC and each other continue through the winding up process. Most state LLC acts permit judicial involvement in the winding up process. Dissolved LLCs can be sued.

Limited Liability Companies and Taxes

Classification as a partnership for federal income tax purposes is one of the critical benefits of the LLC form. Partnership taxation permits the LLC's income, gains, losses, deductions, and credits to flow-through to its members for use on their personal tax returns, thereby permitting a single level of tax. Although corporations also permit limited liability protection to their shareholders, corporate income is generally taxed to the corporation when it is earned, and to the shareholders when distributed as dividends. Similarly, a corporation's losses generally may be used only to offset its income, and do not flow through the corporation for the shareholders' use. Although qualifying small business corporations may elect to be taxed as S corporations, and thereby obtain flow-through tax treatment, partnership taxation frequently is more favorable than taxation pursuant to Subchapter S of the Internal Revenue Code. You should consider the advice of a competent tax professional to guide you through this process.

For self-employment tax purposes, "the distributive share of any item of income or loss of a limited partner, as such, other than guaranteed payments" is excluded from self-employment net earnings. This provision prevents passive investors from qualifying for social security benefits based upon limited partnership investments.

Although the answer is unclear, member-managers and members who otherwise participate in LLC business should be treated as general partners, and their distributive share of LLC income and loss should constitute net earnings from self-employment. On the other hand, the distributive share of income and loss of members who do not participate in LLC business activities (and are therefore similar to investor limited partners) should not constitute net earnings from self-employment. Treasury Regulations are needed to resolve this issue. Resolution of this question will affect the collection of social security taxes, the inclusion of LLC income for coverage purposes, and the treatment of LLC income allocated to a person receiving social security benefits. Again, you should consider the advice of a competent tax professional to guide you through this process.

Overview of Differences and Similarities of Corporations and Limited Liability Companies.

A limited liability company, commonly referred to as an LLC, differs from a corporation in several aspects. First, in a corporation, articles of incorporation are filed with your state's department of commerce or Secretary of State's office. A limited liability company files articles of organization. Corporations, which have been around for hundreds of years, are very rigid in structure and require several formalities as outlined above. A limited liability company does not have as many formal requirements and, rather than having shareholders, has members and may have managers. Similar to a corporation, an LLC's debts and obligations are solely its own and if the limited liability company's formality is maintained and kept, a shield of liability is afforded to them under state law.

One of the formalities required in many states for a limited liability company is that they must have an operating agreement. The operating agreement outlines how the members and/or managers agree to run the company. Usually there is a requirement for at least one annual meeting, and the requirement outlines how actions may be taken without a meeting. Rather than holding stocks of shares, it is common for members to have a percentage of ownership, or a certain member of ownership units to delineate ownership of the LLC.

LLC's are flexible in how they are taxed and how they can pass through directly to the owners, and an LLC may choose to be taxed as an S Corporation with the Internal Revenue Service by filing Form 2553.

What is a "Series LLC"?

A series limited liability company is a special type of LLC. It provides liability protection across multiple fronts, each of which protects from liabilities arising from the others. A series LLC is very much like a corporation in that it is a master LLC with several subsidiaries that operate separately of the master.

The businesses operating through the units may be the same as the master unit or completely different, either of which requires that their individual owners must maintain a separate set of books and records since each has their own assets and liabilities.

Just like a regular LLC, the owners of each section aren't financially responsible for the debts and obligations acquired through their section. The owners of each section are treated by the laws of the state in which the master LLC was created. The owners or members of one unit have no rights as a member of another unit in terms of assets and income. Each section is responsible for its own debts and obligations, which in turn means that creditors of one unit can only reach the assets of that unit and no other.

Management of an LLC

Limited liability companies require that very specific points be adhered to in order to be managed effectively. When you execute an operating agreement, it's essential that its integrity is preserved since the agreement handles the management of an LLC. An operating agreement is required under many state laws for LLCs. Generally, the operating agreement must be very detailed in order for the LLC to run smoothly. So, things like taxation, distribution, lists of any special privileges that are reserved for important members, and an LLC's goals are all outlined clearly and in detail. This helps prevent avoid any confusion or potential future disagreements between members or managers.

Also, it's the managing member's responsibility to make sure that the formation, operation, and maintenance of the LLC is adequately capitalized. Proper capitalization is often closely looked over in courts when the status of your LLC comes under scrutiny, because not having enough capital could be evidence of fraud. This could later be used as a basis to pierce the corporate veil. The managing member also has to make sure that funds aren't being misused, and that the assets of the members aren't being reduced, either excessively or unnecessarily.

Another responsibility of the managing member is to check and prevent any comingling of funds. The personal use of funds, or any use of funds to create an advantage for some members, is permitted. Additionally, having members who are directly responsible for payments for the LLC's debts or financial obligations is not accepted. Such a prohibition might not be for the reason you may assume (that it isn't their responsibility).Rather, it is because the payment of debts and obligations by members eventually leads to your LLC being exposed to allow piercing of the corporate veil and exposing all members of the LLC to individual liability as well as diminishing any protections associated with the LLC.

A proper and inventive management plan is the make-up of a potentially successful LLC, with a good managing member who is the glue that holds those building blocks together. Make sure that all members stick to whatever principles have been outlined in the marketing agreement. Also, be sure to make it very clear to anyone working with you or under you, that personal agendas that don't benefit the LLC as a whole, or even hinders its growth, will not be tolerated. This sort of decision in the ranks can lead to an alter ego determination by courts and can be used against you to pierce the corporate veil. Avoiding liability and unnecessary exposure is best accomplished with proper management. Make sure that your LLC is properly managed to avoid the problems we've discussed herein. Putting your management plan into the operating agreement, or having a management governing document will assure that protections are kept in place and expectations of each member and manager are fully understood.

Chapter **7**

An Overview of Commonly Used Business Forms to Provide Asset Protection

Buy-Sell Agreements

A buy-sell agreement is an agreement made between the owners of a business entity. Through this agreement, the owners consent that in the event that one of the present owners of the company should become disabled, diseased, or die, the other owners may have the opportunity to buy out the interest of the one. This legal instrument can become essential for the transfer of ownership when a dispute arises.

The buy-sell agreement will usually contain provisions that prevent stockowners from selling their interests to anyone in a closely held corporation. This way, the shareholders do not have to work with, or become co-owners with someone they do not get along with or do not approve of. A first right of refusal is usually contained in such an agreement, which allows the current owners to buy out the owner that wishes to withdraw. Proper notice in writing is also required so that the owners are aware of when a shareholder decides to withdraw from the company.

Usually upon the death of an owner of the company, the company then has the right to buy out the ownership of the deceased owner and, upon election of the company not to purchase, the owner along with the shareholders have the right to purchase the shares at a set price. The set price is usually determined by book value, an independent appraisal, or a formula calculated by an independent accountant. Usually terms are allowed where a portion or all payment for the stock is made over a set period, with a fixed rate of interest. This allows the party acquiring the company, sufficient time, and cash flow, to acquire those shares.

If no buy-sell agreement is in place, then the ownership of stock can transfer to the spouse of the deceased, the children of the deceased, or even extended relatives of the deceased, depending on whether the deceased left a will or trust to own those shares of stock. Sometimes, leaving stock to a child of the departed can help them to acquire a step-up in tax basis under the 26 U.S.C. § 1014 which allows the stock to be sold to other shareholders who currently hold interest in the company.

How Having the Proper Documents is Vital to Asset Protection

This was explained earlier; however, it must be emphasized that it is vital for your company to keep and maintain proper records in order to avoid having your company be determined as fraudulent, or to avoid finding that you are not being provided with any asset protection whatsoever. Make sure you keep the company records and documents up-to-date and in proper order.

Your asset protection plan can be extensive depending on your circumstances and your specific asset protection goals; the most important thing you can do is obtain and use competent counsel to assist you with your asset protection plan. These forms can help you avoid problems seen most commonly in the world of asset protection.

Why You Should Have Arbitration Clauses in Your Agreements

Arbitration is a technique used to resolve disputes outside of court. A third party, called the arbitrator, looks over the case, and comes up with a decision that the arbitrator believes is fair for both parties. Arbitration is a form of ADR (alternative dispute resolution).

An arbitration clause is most often used to resolve commercial disputes, usually concerning your business. It is prudent to use arbitration clauses if you want to save money on court costs and attorney fees in the long run, because, should a lawsuit commence regarding your business, it is possible that the lawsuit will last for years. Most times, arbitrations can be resolved, and finality reached within a matter of months.
The interesting thing about an arbitration clause is that it can either be voluntary or involuntary and either binding or non-binding. The distinction between a non-binding arbitration and mediation is that a mediator will try to find a way to compromise, while a non-binding arbitrator is simply removed from the settlement process if one of the parties wants to appeal the arbitrator's decision.

The use of an arbitration clause is more controversial when it comes to consumer and employment cases. The reason for this is, in these instances, arbitration isn't voluntary, and if forced on consumers and employees through the use of fine print, it may result in a court denying an individual his or her rights.

The benefit of having an arbitration clause in your contracts as a business owner is that you can save both time and money when there are disputes settled via arbitration, rather than having a long drawn-out litigation in court. Now, arbitrations are not perfect. Some arbitrators have never been judges, so they might not rule in your favor; however, when it comes to speed and finalization in a dispute, binding arbitration is probably the faster of the methods available.

You can have an arbitration provision that states that any dispute that comes from a contract agreement can be settled by binding arbitration in the state and city where business is being conducted. Each party must pay their own legal fees, and each pays half of the arbitration costs. You can also outline that any judgment made by the arbitrator is binding and final.

The JAMS Foundation and the American Arbitration Association (AAA) are two of the largest arbitration organizations in the United States. Regardless of which association you use, a neutral arbitrator can preside over a non-binding mediation process as well as arbitrations. Items to consider when drafting an arbitration clause include:

- Discovery requests and disputes
- The application and degree of the rules of evidence
- Expert witnesses and cross examinations
- All pertinent evidence
- Arguments for all involved parties
- The settlement of the disputes using the AAA Rules or JAMS Rules

Arbitration clauses can also determine the jurisdiction of the arbitrator. While you can save a lot of time and money, arbitration has its drawbacks just like anything else. If the provisions aren't specified in the contract containing the clause, then the guide for the arbitration is usually ruled to fall under the FAA (Federal Arbitration Act) if there is a federal question. If the arbitrator has a predisposition against your case, you don't have any legal recourse, though as more companies use arbitration as a way to settle their disputes, they bring attorneys to assist them in the process and make appropriate arguments to win their cases.

What are Confidentiality Agreements and Why Should You Use Them?

Nondisclosure agreements, or confidentiality agreements, are contracts between two or more people in which the parties agree to keep certain types of information confidential. These kinds of agreements are used when a company, or individual, has a unique process or a secret product, but which needs the evaluation of another company as a forerunner to a licensing agreement or to review an existing product to come up with a new and different way to make it, market it, or use it.

There are several functions that these agreements perform. Confidentiality agreements:

- Protect sensitive technical or commercial information. If someone outside of the agreement has knowledge of the 'secret,' then there is a breach of contract. The non-breaching party can claim damages and even obtain an injunction.
- Prevent penalty of valuable patent rights and other intellectual property rights. The public disclosure of an invention has the potential to be a forfeit of patent rights.
- Define exactly what sort of information can or can't be revealed by classifying information as confidential.

The type of information protected with a confidentiality agreement is unlimited, and if used correctly, can be used in a dozen ways to increase the assets of your business. You have the potential to gain a competitive advantage when you have a secret that your competitors do not.

Non-Compete Agreements

A non-compete agreement is used in contract law by which an employee agrees not to pursue a similar job or trade, or to open a business which competes with yours. Basically, it's a promise from a former employee who had access to inside knowledge, not to use that knowledge to start a competitive business. This sort of agreement is very effective in protecting your business and corporations from disgruntled or ambitious employees.

Employee Agreements

In the past, an employee agreement was usually reserved for high-profile companies for the benefit of their clients. Now, employee agreements are used all the time in companies to protect the human resource capital of the company. These agreements can help prevent employees from leaving the company early, and prevent them from competing against your company, should they leave employment early.

Employee Agreements should cover the following:

- The job position
- Job description and duties
- Whether the position can be changed by the employer
- The length of the agreement
- Salary, bonus, and benefits
- Whether the employee gets stock or stock options in the company (Oftentimes there is a required vesting period where the employee would earn these over time.)
- When the employee can be terminated for good cause
- What "good cause" means
- When the employee can be terminated without good cause and what severance payment will be due
- The employee's job responsibilities

- The employee's confidentiality obligations
- Where and how disputes will be handled

One potential problem you have to think about when using employee agreements is waiving the employee's "at will" status. In some cases, a company may hire or terminate an employee's relationship "at will." A written employment contract modifies this status and may waive the employer's ability to terminate the employee "at will." Again, it is important to review your state's employment guidelines prior using an employee contract in those states.

What Are Personnel Files and Why Would You Need Them?

Personnel files are a way to keep track of employee's performance history, and in some cases, they can be provided as evidence in lawsuits. These files should be strictly job related, which means that including things about an employee's private life, political beliefs, criticisms, or comments from superiors concerning their race, sex, or religion, are all inappropriate, and can actually be the catalyst for a lawsuit rather than tool needed to get you out of a law suit.

Make sure that your file contains every evaluation the employee has received; review and update the file on an annual basis, make sure that it reflects raises, promotions, and commendations as well as any disciplinary actions that were needed against the employee.

The personnel file needs to be started the day an employee is hired. Any job related documents should be included in the file as well. Including:

- Job description for the position
- Job application and/or resume
- Offer of employment
- IRS Form W-4 (the Employee's Withholding Allowance

Certificate)
- Receipt or signed acknowledgment of employee handbook
- Performance evaluations
- Forms relating to employee benefits
- Forms providing next of kin and emergency contacts
- Complaints from customers and/or coworkers
- Awards or citations for excellent performance
- Records of attendance or completion of training programs
- Warnings and/or other disciplinary actions
- Notes on attendance or tardiness
- Any contract, written agreement, receipt, or acknowledgment
  between the employee and the employer
- Documents relating to the worker's departure

In the end, keeping a personnel file is more about thinking ahead and keeping good records than anything else. Remember, the key is to retain your "paper foxhole," which we discussed earlier in this book, by keeping records of anything material.

Why Should You Have a CPA Do Your Business Tax Returns?

Some CPAs interpret the tax code to benefit the taxpayer, while others will do so in favor of the government. Not only do CPAs know the ins-and-outs of how best to handle business tax returns, but, they can be found everywhere in each state. CPAs have the experience to handle your individual tax needs and business tax needs. CPAs know how the different tax returns coincide with each other. This releases a huge weight from your own shoulders so that you can concentrate on the running of the business rather than the, often confusing, process of tax returns.

Ask any potential CPA how long they've been in the business. Also, ask which employee in their office will be handling your taxes, who will review that employee's work afterwards, and how to contact both. Make sure to ask the CPA how your taxes will be prepared, and if your tax return preparation fees will be calculated. To make sure that your CPA is legitimate, check the licensing board to make sure that they are legally allowed to represent you. Another good place to look is the Better Business Bureau, and your attorney general's office. You can never be too careful when it comes to your money, and when it has to do with taxes, you have to be sure to take even more precautions, or you will suffer the consequences later on.

Why You Need a Good Business Attorney on Your Team

Obviously, any business would need a good business attorney on call to handle any of their legal matters. While some believe it is acceptable to not have an attorney, it does make it more difficult, as well as more expensive, to find one once a situation comes up when one is needed. Attorneys charge a lot less to prevent problems and charge much more to solve them after they show up.

By having a competent business attorney as a part of your team from the beginning, you can establish a relationship. The attorney knows how you run your business, who the people are that run it, and how they operate together. Some may claim that this erases an attorney's objectivity, but in the end, who can better represent your company than someone who knows the ins and outs of it? Your attorney can look over any legal documents that you draw up as well as any that are drawn up for you.

An attorney will be useful in various situations, such as when you are buying a new business and there are environmental issues involved, if an employee decides to sue for something like sexual harassment or discrimination, if your company decides to contribute property to a partnership or LLC, or if you and your partners want to make special allocations of profits/losses in your agreement.

A good business attorney can save your business from certain destruction by making sure your business is run properly, and is in compliance with the law. Truly, having the right business attorney is priceless.

Chapter **8**

An Overview of the Uniform Fraudulent Transfers Act

Because so many asset protection plans involve the transfer of assets, it is often worthwhile to include a discussion of the Uniform Fraudulent Transfer Act (UFTA)[9]. As a state adopts the UFTA, that state law supersedes federal law[10]. Consequently, state specific law is important to an analysis of the UFTA.

All states, except Alaska, have in some form or another, adopted the UFTA. The UFTA defines a "fraudulent transfer" as an exchange or "transfer" of assets made with the intent to defeat the rights of creditors. The fraud element of these transfers allows states to "void" or "reverse" the transaction. This "voiding" or "reversing" allows creditors to satisfy their judgments against an asset improperly transferred by the debtor.

"Void" Transactions

Most states "void" a transaction as fraudulent when creditor demonstrates the debtor had "intent to defraud." The UFTA gives creditors approximately eleven (11) "badges of fraud" to show the debtor's intent[11]. Which "badge" applies, depends on whether the

---

[9] Unif. Fraudulent Transfer Act § 13.
[10] Am. Jur. 2d, Fraudulent Conveyances and Transfers § 4.
[11] Unif. Fraudulent Transfer Act § 4(b).

creditor's claim arose before, concurrently, or after the transfer. Regardless of when the claim arose, creditors are allowed to void transfers on a "constructive fraud theory." A "construction fraud theory" allows the creditor to prove fraud without having to prove actual intent to defraud. Under this theory a creditor may "void" a transfer if the debtor transferred the asset for less than "reasonably equivalent value" or if the debtor intended to incur debts beyond their ability to pay them when they came due[12]. Trust transfers are especially susceptible to this theory because a transfer to a trust is usually not for "reasonably equivalent value."

Creditors can also void transfers by proving the debtor acted with "actual intent to hinder, delay, or defraud[13]." A creditor does not have to prove this intent with regard to the specific creditor making the claim. Rather, a creditor can void a transfer as long as he can show that it was made with the intent to hinder, delay, or defraud any creditor[14]. Furthermore, a creditor does not have to prove actual fraudulent intent since the UFTA lists certain recognized "badges of fraud" from which the court can infer that the debtor made the transfer with the intent to defraud creditors[15]. These "badges of fraud" range from insolvency, transfers to insiders, retention of possession or control by the debtor, and a complete transfer of all of the debtor's assets[16].

The UFTA grants current creditors greater protection than it grants past creditors. For example, a present creditor is able to "void" a transfer without having to show intent, if the transfer is made for less than "a reasonably equivalent value" by a debtor who is insolvent before the transfer is made, or who is made insolvent by the transfer[17]. The UFTA defines insolvency as either the inability of a debtor to pay debts as they become due (the income test), or the circumstance in which the

---

[12] Id

[13] Unif. Fraudulent Transfer Act § 4(a)(1).

[14] Id

[15] Unif. Fraudulent Transfer Act § 4(b)(1) – (11).

[16] Id.

[17] Unif. Fraudulent Transfer Act § 5(a).

value of a debtor's overall debts exceeds the overall value of their assets (the balance sheet test)[18].

A present creditor may also "void" a transfer made by an insolvent debtor in satisfaction of prior debts to "insiders" who have reason to know of the debtor's insolvency[19]. The UTFA defines an "insider" as relatives of the debtor, partnerships where the debtor is a general partner, and corporations of which the debtor is a "director, officer, or person in control."[20] Because of the open nature of the UTFA's definition of an "insider," one could argue the trustee of a self-settled spendthrift trust is an insider if he or she should have known the settlor was insolvent at the time of the transfer.

Statute of Limitations

The statute of limitations for a UFTA claim depends on the basis of the creditor's claim. For example, a creditor attempting to "void" a transfer on the basis of the debtor's "intent to defraud" must bring suit within four (4) years of the time the debtor made the transfer, or from when the original obligation arose. In the case where the creditor is unaware of the transfer, the UFTA allows the creditor to bring an action within one (1) year after the transfer or obligation was, or reasonably could have been, discovered by the creditor[21].

The UFTA gives a creditor four (4) years from the date of the transfer to bring suit when the creditor's claim is based upon the theory of a transfer for less than the "reasonably equivalent value."[22] A creditor only has one (1) year to "void" a transaction based on an allegation of insolvency at the time of a transfer, to satisfy a debt to an "insider."[23] The reason for this short period on insolvency cases is that the UFTA

---

[18] Unif. Fraudulent Transfer Act § 2.
[19] Unif. Fraudulent Transfer Act § 5(b).
[20] Unif. Fraudulent Transfer Act § 1(7)(i).
[21] Unif. Fraudulent Transfer Act § 9(a).
[22] Unif. Fraudulent Transfer Act § 9(b).
[23] Unif. Fraudulent Transfer Act § 9(c).

attempts to balance the need to protect creditors, while also allowing debtors the ability to pay off their oldest debts first. "This philosophy is reflected in an even more striking way with regard to various commercial transactions (for example, transfers made in the ordinary course of business of the debtor and the insider) in which transfers are not voidable at all, even though the transfer itself was fraudulent as to a creditor."

Is it a Good Idea to Transfer Assets From My Estate During Litigation?

The short and simple answer is "no." A transfer of assets during the course of a civil case for the purpose of hindering, delaying or hiding the asset, is referred to as a "fraudulent conveyance." Many state courts will reverse such a conveyance upon a request of a litigant or creditor if the request is made within the statute of limitations and the transfer is truly improper[25].

One of the most prolific examples of fraudulent conveyances is the case of Bernard "Berni" Madoff. In 2009, the United States charged Madoff with conducting a multinational, multibillion dollar Ponzi scheme[26]. Madoff eventually pled guilty to an eleven-count criminal indictment, which leveled charges against him of securities fraud, investment adviser fraud, mail fraud, wire fraud, three counts of international or domestic money laundering, false statements, perjury, false filings with the Securities Exchange Commission (SEC), and theft from an employee benefit plan.

During the course of the litigation, Madoff transferred ownership of several property interests to his wife, Mrs. Ruth Madoff. In a subsequent action, Irving L. Picard, the trustee of Securities Investor.

---

[24] Unif. Fraudulent Transfer Act § 8(f); See also Schurlg, Supplemental Materials for Estate Planning Aspects of Asset Protection Planning, SS008 ALI-ABA 749 (2010).

[25] See Orr v. Kinderhill Corp, 991 F.2d 31, 35 (2nd Cir. 1993).

[26] See U.S. v. Madoff, 626 F. Supp. 2d 420 (S.D.N.Y. 2009); see also See Smith, Madoff Ponzi Scheme Exposes "The Myth of the Sophisticated Investor, 40 U. Balt. L. Rev. 215 (2010).

Protection Corporation (SIPC), was appointed to the Bernard L. Madoff Investment Securities, LLC (BLMIS) case. He alleged that the transfers to Mrs. Madoff, or to entities she controlled or had an interest in, were fraudulent conveyances[27]. Seeking to recover approximately $44.8 million for the benefit of Madoff's defrauded investors, Picard explained that his action was driven by "[T]he inequity between Mrs. Madoff's continuing financial advantages and the economic distress of Madoff's customers." [28]

Picard filed lawsuits to "recover $10.1 billion in fictitious profits paid out by BLMIS," the proceeds of which would be used "to satisfy valid BLMIS customer claims."[29] Although Picard decided not to seek recovery of funds distributed to Madoff investors who suffered a net loss from the fraud, he may seek funds from certain investors whose distributions exceeded their contributions. According to Picard, "[D]ue to the fact that every customer statement was fiction, the first task was to reconstruct the books and records of BLMIS from scratch."[30]
Already, it is apparent that there were no "profits" in the customers' fictitious account statements, but a number of these investors reportedly want a profit anyway. In 2010, U.S. bankruptcy court Judge Burton Lifland ruled in Picard's favor when he confirmed that each investor's respective recovery should not exceed the amounts invested with Madoff, given the "fictitious" nature of the "profits."

In the end, Madoff's wife agreed to surrender her ownership interest in certain property she owned individually or held jointly with her husband. In return, prosecutors agreed not to pursue criminal charges against her. Initially, the Madoffs sought to characterize about $70 million of their assets as "untainted" by Madoff's fraud. The government ultimately allowed Mrs. Madoff to retain about $2.5 million in cash, purportedly unrelated to Madoff's fraud.

---

[27] See Investor Protection Corp. v. Bernard L. Madoff inv. Sec. LLC (In re Bernard L. Madoff Inv. Sec, LLC), 424 B.R. 122, 135 (Bnkr. S.D. N.Y. 2010).
[28] Id.
[29] Id.
[30] Jane J. Kim, As 'Clawback' Suits Loom, Some Investors Seek Cover, Wall St. J., Mar. 12, 2009, at C3, available at http:// online.wsj.com/article/SB123681586212702121.html.

As shown in the Berni Madoff case, individuals must transfer assets to entities with a legitimate and probable business purpose. Transferring assets simply to hide them from creditors, especially during litigation, is not an effective strategy. While it might allow an individual to avoid the occasional lawsuit because a creditor cannot find his or her assets, the strategy may backfire in the end. The bottom line is, if a person transfers an asset simply to avoid creditors, he or she bears a substantial risk of having the court rule the conveyance was fraudulent and may lose the asset.

Chapter **9**

An Overview of Exemptions

 W hen considering asset protection plans, the next step to consider is exemptions[31]. Generally, an exemption is a law that allows certain types of assets to be untouchable by creditors. What determines whether part or all of an asset is untouchable or exempt by statute, depends on the type of asset owned, and what the code states as pertaining to that asset.

Of all exemptions, the most important is probably the homestead exemption. The homestead exemption allows an individual (or couple) an exemption in a certain amount of equity in their property. The following represent a state-by-state list (accurate at the time of printing) of the homestead exemption. It is included for informational purposes only. Do not rely solely on this list. Confirm this information with an appropriate advisor:

---

[31]Ballentine's Law Dictionary defines an exemption as "[a] privilege, sometimes referred to as a right, granted to a debtor by the grace and favor of the state on the grounds of public policy for a humane and generous purpose, which permits him to retain a portion of his property or earnings free from seizure or sale by his creditors under judicial process. 31 Am J2d Exemp §§ 1, 2. Freedom or release from duty or obligation, such as military service or service on a jury, not granted to others indiscriminately. Maine Water Co. v. Waterville, 93 Me 586, 45 A 830; Green v. State, 59 Md 123. An allowance of a deduction in computing net income for tax purposes by way of a personal exemption, an old-age exemption, or a blindness exemption. IRC § 151. The person for whom an exemption may be claimed in an income tax return.

Alabama - Up to $5,000 in value, or up to 160 acres in area

Alaska - Up to $64,800, no area limitation

Arizona - Up to $100,000, no area limitation Arizona Revised Statutes

Arkansas - Up to $2,500 in value, or at least ¼ acre for city homesteads, 80 acres for rural homesteads

California - Up to $50,000 in value.

Colorado - Up to $45,000 in value, no area

Connecticut - Connecticut General Statutes Annotated

Delaware - None

District of Columbia - D. C. provides an exemption equal to owner's aggregate interest in real property (No monetary or area limitations).

Florida - Exemption equal to value of property as assessed for tax purposes (No monetary limitations) –area limitations of ½ acre of urban land or 160 acres of rural land

Georgia - Up to $5,000 in value, no area limitation

Hawaii - Up to $20,000, but the head of a family and persons 65 years of age or older are allowed up to $30,000, no area limitation

Idaho - Up to $50,000 in value, no area limitation

Illinois - Up to $7,500 in value, no area limitation. In cases of multiple owners, can be increased to $15,000

Indiana - Up to $7,500 for a residence, up to $4,000 for additional property, no area limitation. Co-owner, if also a joint debtor, may claim additional $7,500.

Iowa - No monetary limitation, but a minimum value of $500, area limitations of ½ acre of urban land or 40 acres of rural land

Kansas - No monetary limitation - area limitations of 1 acre of urban land or 160 acres of rural land

Kentucky - Up to $5,000 in value, no area limitation

Louisiana - Up to $25,000, but may include entirety of property in cases of catastrophic or terminal illness or injury. Area limitations of 5 acres of urban land or 200 acres of rural land

Maine - Up to $25,000 in value, but may be up to $60,000 under certain circumstances, no area limitation

Maryland - Up to $3,000, but in Title XI bankruptcy proceedings, up to $2,500, no area limitation

Massachusetts - Up to $300,000 in value, no area limitation annotated

Michigan - Up to $3,500 in value - area limitations of 1 acre of urban land or 40 acres of rural land

Minnesota - Up to $200,000 in value, but up to $500,000 if used primarily for agricultural purposes—area limitations of ½ acre of urban land or 160 acres of rural land

Mississippi - Up to $75,000 in value –area limitation of 160 acres

Missouri - Up to $8,000 in value, no area limitation

Montana - Up to $100,000 in value, no area limitation

Nebraska - Up to $12,500 in value –area limitation of 2 lots of urban land or 160 acres of rural land

Nevada - Up to $125,000 in equity, no area limitation

New Hampshire - Up to $50,000 in value, no area limitation

New Jersey - No homestead exemption is provided, but an exemption for personal property of up to $1,000 is allowed

New Mexico - Up to $30,000 in value, no area limitation

New York - Up to $10,000 above liens and encumbrances in value, no area limitation

North Carolina - Up to $10,000 in value, no area limitation

North Dakota - Up to $80,000 in value, no area limitation

Ohio - Up to $5,000 in value, no area limitation

Oklahoma - Unlimited in value –area limitations are 1 acre of urban land or 160 acres of rural land. However, where using more than 25% of property for business purpose, the value drops to $5,000

Oregon - Up to $25,000 in value –area limitations of one city block if within a city or 160 acres of rural land.

Pennsylvania - No homestead exemption provided, but a general monetary exemption of $300 exists.

Rhode Island - Up to $150,000 in value, no area

South Carolina - Although no homestead exemption is provided, an exemption for personal and real property of up to $10,000 in value may include property claimed as a residence.

South Dakota - No monetary limitation - area limitation of one dwelling house and contiguous lots

Tennessee - Up to $5,000, but may be up to $7,500 if claimed by two persons as a homestead, no area limitation

Texas - No monetary limitation –area limitation is 10 acres of urban land or 100 acres of rural land if claimed by a single person. A family may claim 200 acres of rural land

Utah - Up to $20,000 in value, but only $5,000 in value if property is not your primary residence –area limitation of 1 acre

Vermont - Up to $75,000 in value, no area limitation

Virginia - Up to $5,000, but may be increased by $500 for each dependant residing on property, no area limitation

Washington - Generally, up to $40,000 in value, but may be unlimited if used against income taxes on retirement plan benefits, no area limitation

West Virginia - Up to $5,000 in value, but an additional $7,500 may be available in cases of "catastrophic illness or injury," no area limitation

Wisconsin - Up to $40,000 in value, No area limitation

Wyoming - Up to $10,000 in value, each co-owner is entitled to a homestead exemption.

Beyond the homestead exemption, many states offer other types of exemptions. For example, workers compensation benefits are often exempt under the law. Sometimes military property issued to, or owned by a member of the National Guard, is exempt under the law. Also, qualified retirement benefits might be completely exempt under state code.

There are even some business exemptions. For example, certain partnership properties can be exempt. Tools of the trade, implements, or a professional library, can be exempt. A percentage of your earned, but unpaid wages, might also be exempt.

Exemptions can be used to prevent judgment creditors from reaching your exempt assets. Ideally, as you go through this book, you will take an inventory of all of your assets to determine which ones might be exempt, so you will know which assets to address with your legal advisor. You should find a way to shield those assets that are not exempt from potential creditors or lawsuits.

For example, let's say you own a house that is worth $200,000, and you owe $180,000 on the house. This would provide you a net equity of $20,000 in your property. Let us also assume a homestead exemption of $20,000. It will be important for you to keep the home in your personal name, or in the name of a revocable family trust, to take advantage of the homestead exemption. A common mistake people make is placing ownership of the primary residence into an LLC, a corporation, or other business entity. Although this may seem appropriate in order to deter creditors, it would eliminate the exemption that you are provided under state law. Not only will you lose the exemption if you put your primary residence into a corporation or limited liability company, you will also have to pay that entity a monthly payment in order to maintain the corporate veil of that entity and show that it was not a fraudulent transfer. Additionally, other tax benefits are lost when your primary residence is placed into a corporation or an LLC.

Another strategy is to actually record "a declaration of homestead" with the County Recorder's office where the property is located. This will secure and give notice to the entire world that you are taking and claiming an exemption for your primary residence. Additionally, by reviewing the list of exempt assets, you can always liquidate and sell certain assets that are not exempt, and obtain or convert nonexempt assets into assets that are exempt.

Remember also, that when determining which assets to protect and which ones are exempt, it is important to realize how plaintiff's attorneys work. When determining whether to file a lawsuit against you, a plaintiff's attorney will regularly conduct an asset search. This includes going through such systems as Lexis/Nexis, Accurint, Westlaw, Merlin Data, or other asset sources to determine what you own. If the property that you own is not registered, titled, or listed in a certain area, it may be difficult for a plaintiff's attorney to determine whether you have any nonexempt assets worth pursuing. This is important to recognize, and the truth is—if the attorney or party cannot discover what you own, then the plaintiff's attorney may determine that it is not economically feasible to pursue an action against you.

Finally, there are federal exemptions that may be used instead of state exemptions. Additional information regarding these exemptions can be obtained from a competent attorney who regularly practices in asset protection law.

Chapter **10**

An Overview of Bankruptcy

Few individuals consider bankruptcy as a method of asset protection, but in certain circumstances, bankruptcy can provide incredible asset protection opportunities. Furthermore, because bankruptcy can be for individuals as well as businesses, these asset protection opportunities can be extended to both parties. Regardless of whether it is a business or a person filing for bankruptcy, the filing party is often called the "debtor." Defined generally, the debtor is someone who cannot pay their debts.

Bankruptcy offers a degree of solace to debtors seeking relief from the burden of their obligations. On the other hand, it offers some protection to creditors who want an efficient and convenient means to liquidate claims. Most practitioners agree that bankruptcy serves five general purposes: to obtain a discharge, to orchestrate claims, to protect asset (and going concern) values, to provide an opportunity to implement deals, and to give business debtors relief.

For many years, and for most people, bankruptcy meant "the discharge." Most cases were filed by individual debtors who sought to wipe out their past debts, and most of them got what they came for. Debtors had to turn over their non-exempt assets, but most debtors had no non-exempt assets, so it was not a barrier. In other cases, substantial exemptions were provided under state law provisions. For example, as we saw in Chapter Nine, a debtor in Texas could own a million dollar home and claim it as an exemption in his or her bankruptcy. By doing so, the debtor could wipe out all of his creditors and maintain a million dollar asset. Furthermore, and even more sweeping, debtors were able to insulate their post-bankruptcy earnings from pre-bankruptcy claims. That meant that if the debtor filed for bankruptcy on Tuesday, owing a million dollars to his creditors, and then went to Las Vegas on Friday and won a million dollars, his winnings were entirely protected from his pre-bankruptcy creditors.

In 2005, the United States Congress implemented a major overhaul to the Bankruptcy Code. The changes resulted in raising the barrier to entry for individuals seeking bankruptcy protection. This does not mean that the advantages mentioned above disappeared; it just means that it is harder to qualify for those advantages. For example, Congress imposed a "means test" that requires the court to dismiss the cases of some debtors if their prospective earning capacity will yield a surplus that might service past debt. The means test also alters the type of bankruptcy options individuals have. For example, if an individual's income is higher than median average in the county where he or she resides, the individual may not be able to file a chapter 7 bankruptcy. Instead, this debtor may only be able to file a chapter 13 bankruptcy.

Chapter 7 Bankruptcy

Per United States Courts- Section on Chapter 7 http://www.uscourts.gov/FederalCourts/Bankruptcy/BankruptcyBasics/Chapter7.aspx

"A chapter 7 case begins with the debtor filing a petition with the bankruptcy court serving the area where the individual lives or where the business debtor is organized or has its principal place of business or principal assets. (3) In addition to the petition, the debtor must also file with the court: (1) schedules of assets and liabilities; (2) a schedule of current income and expenditures; (3) a statement of financial affairs; and (4) a schedule of executory contracts and unexpired leases. Fed. R. Bankr. P. 1007(b). Debtors must also provide the assigned case trustee with a copy of the tax return or transcripts for the most recent tax year as well as tax returns filed during the case (including tax returns for prior years that had not been filed when the case began). 11 U.S.C. § 521."

"One of the primary purposes of bankruptcy is to discharge certain debts to give an honest individual debtor a "fresh start." The debtor has no liability for discharged debts. In a chapter 7 case, however, a discharge is only available to individual debtors, not to partnerships or corporations. 11 U.S.C. § 727(a)(1). Although an individual chapter 7 case usually results in a discharge of debts, the right to a discharge is not absolute, and some types of debts are not discharged. Moreover, a bankruptcy discharge does not extinguish a lien on property."

"In order to complete the Official Bankruptcy Forms that make up the petition, statement of financial affairs, and schedules, the debtor must provide the following information:
1. A list of all creditors and the amount and nature of their claims;
2. The source, amount, and frequency of the debtor's income;
3. A list of all of the debtor's property; and
4. A detailed list of the debtor's monthly living expenses, i.e., food, clothing, shelter, utilities, taxes, transportation, medicine, etc.

Married individuals must gather this information for their spouse regardless of whether they are filing a joint petition, separate individual petitions, or even if only one spouse is filing. In a situation where only one spouse files, the income and expenses of the non-filing spouse are required so that the court, the trustee and creditors can evaluate the household's financial position."

"Filing a petition under chapter 7 "automatically stays" (stops) most collection actions against the debtor or the debtor's property. 11 U.S.C. § 362. But filing the petition does not stay certain types of actions listed under 11 U.S.C. § 362(b), and the stay may be effective only for a short time in some situations. The stay arises by operation of law and requires no judicial action. As long as the stay is in effect, creditors generally may not initiate or continue lawsuits, wage garnishments, or even telephone calls demanding payments. The bankruptcy clerk gives notice of the bankruptcy case to all creditors whose names and addresses are provided by the debtor."

A chapter 7 bankruptcy filing will discharge all owed pre-bankruptcy debts while liquidating all non-exempt assets. If you live in a state where exemptions are liberal, chapter 7 bankruptcy might be an opportunity to safeguard those assets while removing your creditor's abilities to take them from you.

Chapter 13 Bankruptcy

Per United States Courts- Section on Chapter 13
http://www.uscourts.gov/FederalCourts/Bankruptcy/BankruptcyBasics/Chapter13.aspx

"A chapter 13 bankruptcy is also called a wage earner's plan. It enables individuals with regular income to develop a plan to repay all or part of their debts. Under this chapter, debtors propose a repayment plan to make installments to creditors over three to five years. If the debtor's current monthly income is less than the applicable state median, the plan will be for three years unless the court approves a longer period "for cause." (1) If the debtor's current monthly income is greater than the applicable state median, the plan generally must be for five years. In no case may a plan provide for payments over a period longer than five years. 11 U.S.C. §1322(d). During this time the law forbids creditors from starting or continuing collection efforts."

"Chapter 13 offers individuals a number of advantages over liquidation under chapter 7. Perhaps most significantly, chapter 13 offers individuals an opportunity to save their homes from foreclosure. By filing under this chapter, individuals can stop foreclosure proceedings and may cure delinquent mortgage payments over time. Nevertheless, they must still make all mortgage payments that come due during the chapter 13 plan on time. Another advantage of chapter 13 is that it allows individuals to reschedule secured debts (other than a mortgage for their primary residence) and extend them over the life of the chapter 13 plan. Doing this may lower the payments. Chapter 13 also has a special provision that protects third parties who are liable with the debtor on "consumer debts." This provision may protect co-signers. Finally, chapter 13 acts like a consolidation loan under which the individual makes the plan payments to a chapter 13 trustee who then distributes payments to creditors. Individuals will have no direct contact with creditors while under chapter 13 protection."

"Any individual, even if self-employed or operating an unincorporated business, is eligible for chapter 13 relief as long as the individual's unsecured debts are less than $360,475 and secured debts are less than $1,081,400. 11 U.S.C. § 109(e). These amounts are adjusted periodically to reflect changes in the consumer price index. A corporation or partnership may not be a chapter 13 debtor. Id."

"Filing the petition under chapter 13 "automatically stays" (stops) most collection actions against the debtor or the debtor's property. 11 U.S.C. § 362. Filing the petition does not, however, stay certain types of actions listed under 11 U.S.C. § 362(b), and the stay may be effective only for a short time in some situations. The stay arises by operation of law and requires no judicial action. As long as the stay is in effect, creditors generally may not initiate or continue lawsuits, wage garnishments, or even make telephone calls demanding payments. The bankruptcy clerk gives notice of the bankruptcy case to all creditors whose names and addresses are provided by the debtor."

"Individuals may use a chapter 13 proceeding to save their home from foreclosure. The automatic stay stops the foreclosure proceeding as soon as the individual files the chapter 13 petition. The individual may then bring the past-due payments current over a reasonable period of time. Nevertheless, the debtor may still lose the home if the mortgage company completes the foreclosure sale under state law before the debtor files the petition. 11 U.S.C. § 1322(c). The debtor may also lose the home if he or she fails to make the regular mortgage payments that come due after the chapter 13 filing."

"As a general rule, the discharge releases the debtor from all debts provided for by the plan or disallowed, with the exception of certain debts referenced in 11 U.S.C. § 1328. Debts not discharged in chapter 13 include certain long term obligations (such as a home mortgage), debts for alimony or child support, certain taxes, debts for most government funded or guaranteed educational loans or benefit overpayments, debts arising from death or personal injury caused by driving while intoxicated or under the influence of drugs, and debts for restitution or a criminal fine included in a sentence on the debtor's conviction of a crime. To the extent that they are not fully paid under the chapter 13 plan, the debtor will still be responsible for these debts after the bankruptcy case has concluded."

Beyond Discharge

Filing bankruptcy for the purpose of receiving a discharge is but one purpose of bankruptcy. In some cases, creditors can also use the bankruptcy process to liquidate their claims. Think of it as a kind of "class action," where the creditors get together and appoint a representative to collect the property of the debtor, sell it, and distribute the proceeds. As a matter of history, this "collect and distribute" purpose of bankruptcy precedes "discharge" by several hundred years. It survives today in cases where there are assets to distribute.

When liquidation occurs, the bankruptcy laws provide for distribution on a pro rata basis. What this means is, that after all exemptions are taken, if there is enough to pay 40 percent of all your creditor's claims, the bankruptcy trustee will pay 40 percent of each claim. Pro rata distribution thus supplants a system of "race to the courthouse" that would apply at state law if bankruptcy did not intervene. However, the term pro rata can be misleading because the Bankruptcy Code articulates its own schedule of claim priorities (for administrative expenses, taxes, wages, and so forth). Also, bankruptcy respects the priority positions of those creditors with a valid and perfected security interest (like the mortgage holder on a home). Taken together, even in those relatively few cases where a debtor has assets to distribute, these priority creditors often eat up most of the estate, leaving little or nothing left for the residual class.

Another benefit of bankruptcy is that it offers an opportunity to make and implement deals about a debtor's liabilities and their satisfaction. You often see this in Chapter 11 proceedings, which is a chapter for high net worth individuals and companies wishing to reorganize. Sometimes, it may be in the creditors' interest to settle for less than the full amount they are owed, particularly if they can rely on others to give the same kind of relief. Nothing bars debtors and creditors from making a deal independent of bankruptcy. But, a non-bankruptcy deal may be considerably harder to achieve and harder to enforce than one that is reached through the bankruptcy process.

Why does the bankruptcy process make the deal easier? The most important reason is that the court may impose the terms of the deal on a dissenting minority of creditors. This power to impose may mean the difference between a successful and an unsuccessful deal. It is so important that some plan proponents will make their deal outside bankruptcy and then, if they cannot get unanimous consent, shepherd it through bankruptcy to impose it on dissenters.

Chapter **11**

Ways of Holding Title and How it Impacts Your Asset Protection Plan

There are essentially six distinct ways that you can hold title to property in the United States. The first way is to own something individually— in just your name. This is very common for individuals when they purchase something; it is titled in their name. The last time you purchased a vehicle by yourself, you most likely had it in your name. If you happened to get a loan on the vehicle then it was still titled in your name, and your bank or credit union was recorded as the lender (or lien holder)[32] that financed the purchase.

If you are married and are purchasing something in just your name, usually it will have the distinction as being your sole and separate property from your spouse. It's the same as owning it by yourself, except that by referencing it as your sole and separate property, you are indicating that you have a spouse whom the property is being kept separate from. If you are in a community property estate, one way to further evidence that this property is your sole and separate property is to have the spouse who will not be owning the property, execute a quit claim deed. The deed transfers any right, title, or interest in the property to the other spouse.

A second form of ownership is tenancy in common. A tenant in common is when two or more individuals or entities own one piece of property. Tenants in common may have unequal ownership in the property that is owned. For example, two people might purchase a piece of real estate where one person owns 75% of the property and the other individual owns 25% of the property. The deed would say something to the effect of "Frank Jones as 75% owner and John Smith as 25% owner, as tenants in common." Tenants in common share one unity, which is the right of possession.

Essentially, all of the tenants in common have the right to occupy the property and neither party can exclude the other. This means that if one party decides that they do not want to allow the other party to have possession of the property or enjoy possession of the property, then one party can sue the other in court to have the court either force a sale and liquidation of the property and/or bifurcate the property if possible.

A third manner of ownership is joint tenancy. Generally, any real property that is purchased by a couple as husband and wife is presumed to be joint tenancy. Joint tenancy is where two or more people own 100% of the property and, when one of those individuals or entities ceases to exist, the others continue to own 100% of the property.

 Joint tenancy requires the four unities of time, title, interest, and possession. This means that each owner must receive the title at the same time, and on the same deed or document which evidences ownership, each owner must also have the same undivided 100% interest in the property, as well as identical rights of possession in the property.

A joint tenancy is preferred between spouses in an effort to avoid probate by allowing the individual spouse to obtain the property by operation of law rather than probating the estate or administering trust. Joint tenancy is extremely different from being tenants in common, in that the latter allows owners to have unequal ownership of the property.

All owners in a joint tenancy have 100% ownership at the same time. Joint tenancy is as common between a parent and child as it is between a husband and wife. It also occurs on occasion between unrelated parties for business interests, but is usually only used between family members.

Personal property can also be held in joint tenancy. For example, if you have a joint bank account with your spouse or a stock brokerage account, you will see the letters J.T.W.R.O.S., which stands for "Joint Tenants With Rights Of Survivorship."

Regardless of whether the term 'with rights of survivorship' is contained on the title or not, the simple phrase "joint tenancy" has the same effect. Some states are more liberal and allow John Doe and Jane Doe to be considered joint tenants with rights of survivorship. However, the best practice is to always list the term in joint tenancy or 'as joint tenants' to delineate specifically what your intentions are in regards to that property.

Some statutes automatically provide that joint tenancy is presumed by husband and wife in any granting documents. A granting document in this case would be considered a deed representing ownership of real property.

A fourth manner of ownership is through community property. As noted above, only married people may hold title in community property. Community property is based on state law and not how property is titled.

The fifth way to hold title is through a legal entity. A legal entity is considered a corporation, a limited liability company, a partnership, or a limited partnership, which is jointly referred to as a 'company' in this section. As previously explained, a company can own real estate and other personal property just as a living breathing human being can. If a company owns title to a property, it can also be a joint tenant or a tenant in common, as long as the required unities are in place.

Depending on where the real property or personal property is located, you may or may not want to transfer property into a company. Sometimes there is no property transfer tax. Therefore, there is no negative tax implication for real property, should you place your property into a company.

However, this is not so for all states. For example, in the state of California, transferring property into a company will cause a reassessment of the property tax value, which will usually result in an increase of property taxes. What that ultimately means is that great care should be taken when determining whether to transfer real property in your state from yourself into a company. Seeking competent legal advice to avoid any tax reassessments or using a competent professional to prevent other unforeseen problems is always recommended.

The sixth way to hold title is through a trust. A trust is similar to a company, in that it is a fictitious legal entity that only exists in the contemplation of law. One of the benefits of owning a property in a trust instead of in an individual's name is that it does not go through probate when the individual passes away. There are several different types of trusts which will be addressed in another chapter. It is important to know that a trust may not only be a great estate planning tool, but also an asset protection tool in order to protect real estate and other property from creditors.

Chapter **12**

Protecting Yourself and Your Spouse

W hen considering asset protection for your spouse, you should consider the marital laws in the state in which you live. In the western half of the United States, there are some community property states. Community property states are states where everything purchased or owned by one spouse while a couple is married, is considered property of the marital community. At the time of this writing, there are nine states that are community property states including Arizona, California, Idaho, Louisiana, Nevada, New Mexico, Texas, Washington and Wisconsin. All other states in the U.S. are considered separate property states.

Generally, separate property means that the creditor of one spouse cannot sue or collect from the separate property of the other spouse. In order to explain this in better detail, let's look at the following example:

Henry and Wilma get married in their early twenties. Henry goes to medical school and becomes a doctor. During their marriage, Henry starts a medical practice and purchases a building where he can run his medical practice. He purchases the building in his name and he signs for the loan. Wilma, his wife, never goes to medical school and never participates in the business, nor does she intend to become a nurse or doctor. Henry gets sued and eventually a creditor obtains a judgment against him. Wilma, of course, owns the marital home herself since it is not in Henry's name. Can the creditor place the judgment against Wilma's home?

In a state where the property owned by Wilma is separate property it will be recognized as hers and hers alone. Henry does not have an interest or ownership in that property and therefore, the creditor would not be able to go after the personal residence. However, the creditor could go after the building owned by Henry because it is in his name and he signed for the loan on the building, which makes him the sole owner.

One of the benefits of living in a state where separate property is recognized is that property can be titled in the name of either spouse and, therefore, reduces the exposure. This in turn, protects certain assets. The easiest way to do this is to simply title certain assets with the spouse who has the lowest risk or lowest exposure. There are better, more advanced asset protection strategies, but this is a simple, cost-effective method for reducing exposure from a high-risk spouse.

There still is an issue for the lower risk spouse. If he or she got into a horrible automobile accident and insurance wasn't sufficient to cover the losses suffered by the victims, then all of the assets titled in the lower risk spouse's name would then become susceptible to a judgment. So although this strategy can work, there are complications with it as well. In order to prevent this, a family limited partnership, LLC, Corporation, or trust is preferable to shield that asset from liability.

Important Things to Know About Community Property

There are some essential things about community property you should know, even if you live in a state where community property is not recognized. The first thing you should realize is that if you acquire real estate in a state that has community property laws, then those community property laws apply to that property. This means that if you and your spouse were to purchase property in California and you live in the state of Alabama, regardless of how that real property is titled on the deed, it is technically property of the community estate, meaning that half of it is owned by the husband, and half by the wife.

If you attempted to put real property into a community property state in the name of one spouse during the course of the marriage, it is still considered community property, and other asset protection strategies should be employed instead of just titling property in the lower risk spouse's name.

Essentially, any property that is acquired by spouses during their marriage is presumed to be community property, but property that was owned by a spouse prior to marriage and brought into marriage remains that spouse's separate property. A known exception to the community property rule is that when property is acquired by a spouse during marriage, either by gift or by inheritance, and that separate property consistently remains in only one spouse's name, that property is separate property.

Community property laws vary from state to state, but essentially, they affirm that if your wife's father passes away and leaves her $100,000, that $100,000 does not become community property but instead remains your wife's property alone, separate from you.

How Do Creditors See Community Property?

One of my first law clerk positions during law school was with a firm that represented Sears Roebuck and Company, which collected unpaid debt on Sear's credit cards. We were located in a community property state. In my experience as a law clerk, we would regularly file suit, not only against the individual that incurred the debt on the card, but also against his or her spouse. We would list them as a Jane Doe or a John Doe in the pleading and while we were at it, we'd also sue the community estate.

Often, we did not know whether an individual was married or not. However, in an abundance of caution we would also sue their spouse in case they had performed this type of asset protection. Obviously, in a community property state if property is owned by the community (meaning that one half is owned by the husband and the other half is owned by the wife), then the creditor is able to collect from either spouse because all property is owned by the community estate. Legally speaking, this allows the creditor to collect a judgment from either spouse or whoever holds the assets. The creditor, once they obtain a judgment, can literally choose from which party it wants to collect.

This means that any property that is community property should utilize another asset protection strategies. Additionally, if you live in a community property state or have ever lived in a community property state, it would benefit you to seek competent legal advice as to how you should title your assets in order to properly protect them.

Prenuptial Agreements and Postnuptial Agreements

There are several reasons why you may want to consider having a marital agreement, especially if you live in a separate property state. A marital agreement outlines, at the time of its execution, what happens to certain personal property and real property as of the date of the document. It can outline ownership of the items of property as well as each spouse's rights to that property. In a marital agreement, you can change the ownership rights of certain property and protect certain assets, as well as protect children of the marriage.

 In order for a marital agreement to be legally binding, usually the agreement should include all of the property of both of the spouses, whether pre or post-nuptial. Each spouse must have their own attorney sign the document and have it notarized, or at least have the opportunity to do so.

Something to consider in this type of agreement is who is entitled to what personal property. This might apply to family heirlooms or other items of significant value that are owned before or during the marriage. Although the spouses may never get a divorce, it is prudent to take the opportunity to delineate who should get what, and then put the decision in writing. The document can also outline family businesses, real estate owned by spouses; protect the inheritances of children from a prior marriage, and any retirement benefits belonging to one of the spouses.

The marital agreement will modify the state law as to any property outlined and addressed in the marital agreement, and can state that whatever the wife brought into the marriage belongs to the wife and whatever the husband brought into the marriage belongs to the husband. It may also state that any property acquired by the husband during marriage is his property and any property acquired by the wife during marriage is her property. A properly drafted marital agreement will make it clear that each spouse is responsible for only that spouse's income, assets, and other property; and so long as there is no co-mingling of any property, the marriage will never have community property unless this process is altered.

An example of how a marital agreement might benefit you and your spouse would look something like this:

> Let's say that John and Jane Doe have been married for four years and John has started a contracting business. The business becomes quite successful and requires a lot of heavy equipment. The economy takes a sudden downturn, and John is in a position where some of his equipment is paid off and some is not. John is unable to continue making payments on the financed equipment, and is looking for a way to transfer the equipment to his wife.

> His wife sets up a limited liability company and purchases all the equipment that is paid in full and then leases it to the construction company that is owned by John. John and Jane have a marital agreement which outlines that his company is his and that the

holding company is hers. This method can work as long as there is not a fraudulent transfer to keep the financing company or any other creditor from coming after the equipment that was previously owned by John's construction company.

As in this scenario, a marital agreement can specifically delineate that all of the company's equipment is owned by one individual spouse and, therefore, any other spouse has no right, title, interest, or claim to that property. The downside of this strategy is if the couple ever gets divorced, Jane would be able to take all of the equipment that is paid for, and liquidate that company. John would have no right to obtain any proceeds from her liquidation. When using this type of asset protection plan, it is essential that the spouses trust each other and not take advantage of each other. Otherwise, they should use a different strategy.

Should I Transfer All Of My Assets to My Spouse?

Transferring everything in a marital agreement from one spouse to the other is probably not a great strategy for several reasons. By transferring all assets from one spouse to the other, especially if it's done within the last two years prior to a lawsuit, would indicate a potential fraudulent transfer. It could also show a blatant attempt to hinder or delay creditors. A better plan would be transferring approximately 50% to 75% of marital property from one spouse to the other, depending on what the couple owns and what types of assets are being transferred. The more specific the situation, the better the legal advice will be.

Let's look at John and Jane Doe for a minute. John is the sole owner of his construction company. His construction company is not going to be an exempt asset (even if it is a corporation or LLC). If John Doe wanted to retire, he could sell his construction company to another entrepreneur or general contractor.

We know that the company or corporation has a fair market value that can be assessed by either book value or by obtaining an independent appraisal. That company may have value to a new contractor. However, a creditor would really see no value in that business because without John Doe, the business might not continue.

A license is required in order to be a contractor, and John Doe has probably built a relationship with the people he works with and has contracts with them. If John Doe sold the construction company to another contractor, it is very possible that the new contractor would want John Doe to enter into a non-compete agreement, which would prevent John Doe from entering into another business and competing with him. Without any actual equipment or other assets owned by John Doe's construction company, the company isn't worth a whole lot.

Although the construction company is an asset that has value, that value isn't much, which means that creditors would be uninterested in ceasing it or having it liquidated if there is nothing they could auction off for money.

In order to facilitate this strategy, any equipment could be transferred to a new company with new owners and leased to John Doe's construction company; however, property should not be moved to Jane Doe in this situation because John is the one that holds the license and he is the one at a higher risk. Transferring some assets owned by that company to a company owned by Jane Doe might be a good strategy, but Jane Doe should not own any part or portion of John Doe's construction company.

Should we consider transferring John Doe's 401K, which contains $400,000, to his wife Jane? The answer is simple. In many states, a qualified retirement plan has an unlimited exemption value. Therefore, no creditor could obtain those funds since they are exempt assets, which means that there is no need to transfer any retirement benefits from one spouse to the other.

What about transferring the personal residence of Mr. and Mrs. Doe? In this hypothetical example, Jane Doe is a homemaker. She does not engage in any business activities outside of the home other than owning the limited liability company that leases equipment to John Doe's construction company. In this example, it would be a good idea to transfer some of the marital property from both John and Jane Doe to just Jane Doe. An additional asset protection step would be to have Jane Doe transfer that property from her name into a trust or other entity, depending on the asset.

Based on this example, it is clear that using a marital agreement to delineate which assets belong to each spouse may be a good idea but it is not the end all solution in an asset protection strategy, nor is it the end of the asset protection planning.

John and Jane Doe could heighten the protection of their assets by placing rental properties that they both own, into limited liability companies to shield them from creditors and other exposure. Additionally, they could place their personal residence into a qualified residence trust, create a revocable living trust for each spouse, and possibly create a family limited partnership, depending on their children.

Chapter **13**

What is a Charging Order?

There are relatively few types of assets which are statutorily protected from claims of creditors. For example, partnership interests and membership interests in limited liability companies (LLCs) are afforded a significant level of protection through a charging order.

A charging order creates these protections. Before the advent of the charging order, a creditor pursuing a partner in a partnership was able to obtain from the court a writ of execution directly against the partnership's assets, which led to the seizure of such assets by the sheriff. This result was possible because the partnership itself was not treated as a juridical person, but simply as an aggregate of its partners.

The seizure of partnership assets meant that the sheriff could shut down the partnership's place of business. This shut down would cause the non-debtor partners to suffer financial losses, which often were equal or greater than the debtor partner's debt[33].

Not surprisingly, non-debtor partners began to petition the courts for change due to the great harm they suffered when a creditor exercised his or her rights to seize the debtor partner's interest in the partnership. Non-debtor partners also argued that a partnership is a legal entity separate and distinct from the individual, and not simply an aggregate

---

[33] Brown, Janson & Co. v. A. Hutchinson & Co., 1895 Q.B. 737 (Eng. C.A.).

[34] Because a charging order limits a creditor's remedies, the benefit to the debtor is considered as an asset protection tool. Over the years, the charging order protection was extended to limited partners and LLC members.

of the partners. These concerns could be satisfied only by limiting the collection remedies that creditors previously enjoyed. Two results arose from these circumstances: partnerships were treated as distinct and independent entities, and the charging order was born[34].

Charging orders first appeared in the English Partnership Act of 1895, and in Section 28 of the United States Uniform Partnership Act of 1914 (UPA)[35]. The UPA allowed creditors to petition the court for an order against a debtor's partnership interest. In 1976, the UPA was amended as the Uniform Limited Partnership Act (ULPA). The amendment clarified the charging order and provided that a creditor had a right to the debtor's partnership interests. A couple of other acts, the Revised Uniform Partnership Act of 1994 (RUPA), and the Uniform Limited Liability Company Act of 1996 (ULLCA), further clarified this issue.

These uniform acts make four important points. First, a charging order is a lien on the judgment debtor's transferable/distributional interest; it is not a levy. Second, a creditor cannot exercise any management or voting rights because the creditor has only the rights of an assignee/transferee. Third, the foreclosure of the charged interest does not harm the debtor because the buyer at the foreclosure sale receives no greater right than was possessed by the original creditor. Lastly, a creditor, expressly, has no remedy other than the charging order and foreclosure on the charging order.

In particular, because a charging order creates a lien and not a levy and because a creditor is not a transferee under ULPA but has only the rights of a transferee, a creditor does not become the owner of the charged interest unless there is a foreclosure.[36]

---

[35]Uniform Partnership Act § 28 (1914).
[36]See Stein, Building Stumbling Blocks: A Practical Take On Charging Orders, 8 No. 5 Busent 28 (2006).
[37]See Internal Revenue Code § 177.

Charging orders also deter creditors from initiating lawsuits because of the taxable consequences of obtaining a judgment against a legal entity from whom the creditor is unable to collect[37]. Pursuant to IRC Section 177, a creditor who obtains a judgment against a legal entity must pay taxes on the judgment irrespective of whether or not he or she is able to collect the judgment from the debtor's legal entity or trust. The risk of a tax detriment without benefit deters creditors from seeking judgments from debtors who have legal entities or trusts in jurisdictions which have favorable charging orders.

Which Court Has Authority to Enter a Charging Order?

A state court must have competent jurisdiction before it may enter a charging order against a partnership or LLC. What constitutes a competent jurisdiction varies. A court has jurisdiction if the state has personal jurisdiction over a member, the state has jurisdiction over the membership interest, or the state has personal jurisdiction over the partnership or LLC.[38]

Personal Jurisdiction Over a Member or Partner

Personal jurisdiction exists if the entity or asset has sufficient contacts in the state claiming to have jurisdiction. Generally, a state's "long arm" statute helps set forth which individuals or entities have sufficient contact with the state to establish personal jurisdiction. A partnership or LLC may disregard a charging order obtained in a state that does not have personal jurisdiction over the matter. This is true even if the charging order is domesticated in a state which has personal

---

[37]See Internal Revenue Code § 177.
[38]See Feinberg v. Feinberg, 924 S.W.2d 328 (Mo. App., 1996).

jurisdiction. In cases where the creditor obtained a charging order in a state without personal jurisdiction, the creditor is forced to domesticate the judgment in the state where the LLC or partnership was formed, and seek a charging order from a court in that state.

Recent case law, however, suggests personal jurisdiction exists for an entire partnership or LLC as long as the state has personal jurisdiction over one partner or member[39]. In Hotel 71, the New York Court of Appeals held that since a New York court had personal jurisdiction over a defendant nonresident LLC member, the defendant's personal property, including 22 LLC interests, was subject to attachment in New York.

Personal Jurisdiction Over A Membership Interest

Another way to establish personal jurisdiction over an entity in order to obtain a charging order, is to show that the state has personal jurisdiction over the membership interest and not the LLC. In this case, the location of LLC membership interest governs the jurisdictional outcome. In particular, a judgment creditor may seek a charging order in the jurisdiction where the entity or partnership is located[40].

Personal Jurisdiction Over an Entity Formed Under the Laws of That Jurisdiction

Since a partnership or LLC membership interest is intangible personal property, it must be 'located' somewhere, and the proper location is the state where the partnership or LLC was created[41]. The most permissive view requires only personal jurisdiction over the debtor member. If the LLC is not an indispensable party to the charging action, the order will be respected in the LLC state of formation. This is true even if the court order from another state must first be domesticated in the state of formation.

---

[39]Hotel 71 Mezz. Lender LLC v. Falor, 2010 N.Y. Slip Op. 01348 (N.Y. Ct. App., 2010).
[40]See Koh v. Inno-Pac. Holdings, Ltd., 54 P.3d 1270 (Wash. App. 2002).
[41]See Del. Code Ann. 6, § 18-703(f).

A judgment creditor may only enforce a charging order obtained from a court, which has personal jurisdiction over the partnership or LLC. Generally, personal jurisdiction over a partnership or LLC exists if the state has personal jurisdiction over a member, the state has jurisdiction over the membership interest, or the state has personal jurisdiction over the partnership or LLC.

After a Creditor Obtains a Charging Order, What Can They Do with It?

Distributions

A charging order is relatively uniform in mechanics and effect. As mentioned, any judgment creditor of a member of an LLC, a partner, or a partnership, may seek a charging order from a court with jurisdiction to collect an unsatisfied judgment[42]. Again, the entry of the order creates a judicial lien against the partnership or LLC interest[43]. Like a garnishment order, a charging order requires the LLC to pay any distributions that would 'otherwise be paid' to the judgment debtor, directly to the judgment creditor[44].

In other words, the entry of a charging order does not require the partnership or LLC to declare and pay any distributions; it simply redirects actual distributions to the judgment creditor. Thus, if the entity does not make any distributions, the judgment creditor gets nothing. In a few states, to effectuate collection of distributions pursuant to the charging order, the court may also appoint a receiver over the assets with power to make distributions[45]. These additional powers are not uniform among the states, and in most cases, the judgment debtor continues to enjoy any exemptions from collection that otherwise exist.

---

[42]See Del. Code Ann. 6, § 18-703(a) (1999); Cal. Corp. Code § 17302(a) (2006); and N.Y. Limited Liability Company Law § 607(a) (McKinney 2007).
[43]Unif. Ltd. Liab. Co. Act § 503(a) (2006).
[44]Id.
[45]Ten states authorize the appointment of a receiver including California, Hawaii, Idaho, Iowa, Kentucky, Montana, South Carolina, Utah, Vermont, and West Virginia. See Bishop, LLC Charging Orders: A Jurisdictional and Governing Law Quagmire, n. 25, 12 No. 3 BUSENT 14 (2010).

Foreclosure

Partnerships, LLCs, and trust law are sharply divided about whether or not a judgment creditor may seek to foreclose its charging order lien through a judicial sale of the charged LLC membership interest.

The UPA of 1914 did not specifically authorize foreclosure, but it expressly provided that an "interest charged may be redeemed at any time before foreclosure, or in case of a sale being directed by the court may be purchased without thereby causing a dissolution[46]." Therefore, the concept of foreclosure was contemplated if the distributions under the charging order were inadequate to satisfy the judgment within a reasonable time[47]. The ULPA of 1916 has a similar provision and case law has used RULPA to allow a creditor to foreclose against a partnership interest[48]. Both RUPA and ULPA appear to authorize foreclosure[49].

The Revised Uniform Limited Liability Company Act of 2006 ("RULLCA"), however, clarified that the foreclosure of a charging order lien is available only on a showing that distributions under a charging order will not pay the judgment debt within a reasonable time[50]. The purchaser, however, never retains an ownership interest, but just a transferable interest in the LLC[51].

---

[46]Unif. Partnership Act § 28(2) (1914).

[47]Gose, The Charging Order Under the Uniform Partnership Act, 28 Wash. L. Rev. 1 (1953).

[48]Unif. Ltd. Partnership Act § 22 (1916); Crocker Nat'l Bank v. Perronton, 255 Cal. Rptr. 794 (Cal.   Ct. App., 1989).

[49]See Rev. Unif. Partnership Act § 504(b) (1997); Unif. Ltd. Partnership Act § 703(a).

[50]Rev. Unif. Ltd. Liab. Co. Act. § 503(c).

[51]Id.

State law, where the partnership or LLC is created, will govern whether or not a creditor is able to foreclose on a charging order. For example, Alaska, Georgia, New Jersey, South Dakota, and Texas laws expressly preclude foreclosure in all events[52]. Additionally, Delaware, Nevada, and Virginia have removed the statutory right to foreclose on a charging order lien, leaving their statutes silent in regard to foreclosure.[53] The removal of the express foreclosure provisions indicates that foreclosure is also precluded in these jurisdictions.

Equitable Remedies

In most cases, where the foreclosure of a charging order lien is precluded by statute, a judgment creditor will be confined to a charging order. The exclusive remedy provisions of the charging order statute will render attempts to use other collection procedures ineffective. Two equitable remedies exist which may allow a judgment creditor to access the entities assets: statutory dissolution and common law reverse piercing.

---

[52]Alaska Stat. § 10.50.380(c) (2008); Ga. Code Ann. § 14-11-504(b) (2003 & Supp. 2009); N.J. Rev. Stat. § 42:2B-45 (West 2004); S.D. Codified Laws § 47-34A-504(e) (2007 & Supp. 2009).
[53]Del. Code Ann. 6, § 18-703 (1999); Nev. Rev. Stat. § 86.401 (2004); and Va. Code Ann. § 13.1-1041.1 (2006). Of the remaining states, twelve (12) expressly permit foreclosure of the charging order lien and thirty (30), including the District of Columbia; do not mention foreclosure in any way.
[54]Rev. Unif. Ltd. Liab. Co. Act § 409.

Statutory Dissolution

Statutory dissolution exists when the jurisdiction forces the entity to dissolve for failure to follow corporate or partnership governance. The hope is that the entity will make a distribution at dissolution, allowing the judgment creditor to satisfy his or her charging order lien. This remedy, however, is often times fruitless to the creditor because, even in dissolution, the LLC owes no duty to declare and pay distributions to members or transferees, let alone a judgment creditor[54]. In any case, judicial dissolution is extremely rare.

Reverse Piercing

The remaining opportunity to correct inequitable abuses of power by those in control of the LLC includes the equitable doctrine of reverse piercing. Under this doctrine, the creditor of a partner or member seeks to enforce the partner's or member's debts against the partnership or LLC. In the context of a multi-member LLC, this "remedy" is remote since its application encumbers the non-debtor partner's and member's interest.

The preclusion and/or silence of statutory foreclosure provisions limits a judgment creditor's ability to reverse pierce an entity. For the most part, these judgment creditors are generally unsecured creditors without the power and right of a secured creditor under UCC Article 9 to enforce their security interests. Creditors with secured rights are affected differently by anti-foreclosure restrictions. Thus, preclusion primarily affects unsecured judgment creditors. This means that a creditor who obtains an advance security interest in a partnership or LLC membership interest has far superior rights than an unsecured judgment creditor. Generally, the unsecured creditor status is the result of a tort judgment.

The variance of state laws regarding charging order liens and the right to foreclose along with sparse case laws creates several dilemmas for creditors attempting to satisfy a judgment. With states such as Alaska and Delaware expressly prohibiting foreclosure of charging order liens, creditors are finding it increasingly difficult to pierce the protective shields of a partnership or LLC. The key, as always, is to select a jurisdiction that has favorable charging order legislation and case law.

Chapter **14**

Asset Protection with Insurance

The problem that most people have when it comes to insurance is that the protection provided is often never enough to cover their individual needs. This means that worries that were supposed to be taken care of with that first insurance purchase are now still hovering over their head. The worries end up being even greater than they were before, because now they have to either come up with more money to take care of those worries, or just blindly hope that a situation won't arise where you would need it.

Starting and running a corporation or business, or even managing your everyday personal life, is stressful enough that you shouldn't have to worry about insufficient insurance when you believed that it was taken care of.

Before buying insurance, the first things to take into account are your individual needs and what forms of insurance would best fit what you're looking for. You might want to look into both term life and whole life insurance and when you do, make sure that you've also considered the current inflation rates and rising costs in comparison to your debts (unpaid mortgage, credit cards, and loans). Now consider any hidden income you have, such as perks and employment contributions to your 401(k) plan.

Insurance policies change state by state, and what may be covered in one form of insurance in one state may not be covered in another state. When all of that is determined, you can move on to calculating the amount of coverage you need. The consensus is that your coverage should be at least 10 to 20 times the amount of your annual income.

However, because the amount of insurance needed varies so widely from one person to the next, it is best to be safe rather than sorry. In the end, your insurance should be more than your net worth. It may seem like a lot, but when you factor in all the variables, what seemed like a fortune at first will only last a few years in the end.

You should also have your policies reviewed annually by an insurance agent that is an expert in the field. You should have your insurance reviewed especially when there are significant changes in your life. Such changes may include the arrival of a new baby, a death, an increase in income, an upgrade in assets such as any vehicles, expensive jewelry, tools, machinery, or other acquired assets. Just because you thought of everything when the policy was first bought, doesn't mean that you'll never have to consider these things again. Every time something changes, your policy should be looked over and updated if necessary, to make sure that you're prepared under any circumstances.

What is a CGL policy and why might you need one?

A commercial general liability policy can be useful in many ways to protect your employees and business. The insurance that you currently have for your general liability, your property, and your company may not be adequate to protect you from as much as you think.

With a commercial general liability policy, or a CGL policy, you are protected against claims of property damages, bodily injury, and a host of various liability lawsuits. The CGL it isn't just for you; this sort of policy is perfect for small businesses because it covers a contingent of potential disasters.

Say for instance that you have a joint venture with another company, or your own business is a partnership. Not only does the CGL cover all of the partners, members, and their spouses in case of a lawsuit garnered from their acting on behalf of the business, but if your business is a corporation or association, all of the executives, volunteers, directors, and stockholders are covered, as well.

If you happen to own more than 50% of the stock in a subsidiary, the CGL policy will offer extended coverage. If you have a written agreement with someone (e.g. a vendor) whom you are supposed to be covering, then the CGL policy will protect them against any liability claims they may receive from the distribution of your product; just as any legal representatives will be protected for liabilities arising from the maintenance of your product.

A CGL protects your employees and anyone else who is associated with your business where regular insurance policies will not. You should consult with an expert insurance agent to decide whether a CGL policy is right for you and your business.

What is an Umbrella Insurance Policy and Why Might You Need One?

An Umbrella Insurance Policy is a form of coverage that goes beyond the normal limits set up for homes, auto, boats, or other motor vehicles. Umbrella insurance protects against vandalism, libel, slander and invasion of privacy, while also providing added liability protection for individuals at risk of being sued for damage to someone else's property. This is especially true if the individuals that are being sued happened to have a lot of assets, and are therefore, more likely to be sued.

The premium for this sort of policy can be less expensive if bought from the same insurance agency that provides you with your auto, home, and business insurance, though in some cases like home or auto, it's necessary to have basic insurance coverage before you can qualify for an umbrella policy.

The reason umbrella policies are so essential for any company is, that much like their name, they fill the holes and gaps in your coverage. An umbrella policy can often be seen in situations where you've been sued under your auto insurance policy, if someone is injured on your property and you're sued under your homeowners insurance, or in the event of a natural disaster where a piece of your property (like a tree) damages your neighbors home or car.

Americans suffer from lawsuit happy attitudes. You don't want to lose your assets and potentially your business simply because someone gets hurt and there is a gap in your current coverage. Protecting yourself from gaps is one of the smartest things you can do for yourself and your business.

Chapter **15**

An Asset Protection Example

I think that the best way to learn is by example. So, in order to outline an advanced asset protection plan, we will do so through a hypothetical example. This example will show some of the techniques outlined in this book and others that are more advanced and have not been addressed in this book.

Henry and Wilma live in Utah. They have been married for twenty years and have (through Henry's automotive repair business) acquired several assets. They have three houses (one primary residence and two rental properties); four motor vehicles (two trucks and two sedans); Wilma has some jewelry; Henry has a coin collection worth about $1,000; they have a combined total of $175,000 in two Roth IRAs; they have $6,000 in their checking account and $10,000 in a savings account. Because life has been good over the years, they have also spent money on nice vacations and other items, ringing up about $40,000 in credit card debt.

Unfortunately, the economic downturn over the last few years has hurt Henry's business and he has had to close his repair shop. Henry and Wilma begin to live off of their savings. They sell Henry's coin collection to pay bills and the money they once had is diminishing each day. Henry is discouraged. Wilma is distraught. They seek asset protection advice. What should the plan be?

The first step is to stop the leaks and protect what they have, not only from attack, but to prevent loss in a possible future bankruptcy case, depending on how things go. First, we need to know how much Henry owes on the primary residence.

It is worth $250,000 and they still owe $210,000 on it. What is the strategy here? Leave it alone – there is a total of $40,000 exemption allowed on your personal residence under Utah state law.

If the rental properties pay for themselves or if they have positive cash flow, they can keep the rentals. If they are negative, Henry and Wilma should let the rentals go by either putting them on the market for sale or allowing them to go into foreclosure, depending on the circumstances. Short sales are options depending on how upside down the houses are. Even if they have equity, it does not make sense for Henry and Wilma to get more and more behind each day. Remember: plug those holes.

Vehicles – Depending on the entity that Henry has, the trucks might be in his corporation or LLC. We need to find out if there is debt on the vehicles and then advise him what to do with them. The work vehicles should be protected in a company, and the sedans can be put in the family limited partnership or the family trust, depending on when Henry and Wilma intend on selling or replacing them.

IRAs – They are exempt under Utah State law, so we would leave them alone and not change their ownership. If Henry and Wilma wanted to take control of their investing, they could convert the IRA into a self-directed IRA, invest the money into real estate (perhaps the rental properties), and make into cash flow. If this happened, then LLCs or asset protection trusts would need to be created for the rental properties, to avoid unnecessary liability.

Jewelry – Wilma's jewelry would need to be appraised to make sure it is under the $1,000 exemption limit. If it is, the jewelry could be put into the FLP or family trust. If it is not, Wilma should consider exchanging the jewelry for an exempt asset or, if possible, turn it into an investment or partnership property to avoid the exposure.

Checking and Savings – Henry and Wilma should use the money they have to live on and pay their bills. They should pay secure debts first, priority debts second, and unsecured debts last.

Chapter **16**

Foreign Corporations

Individuals utilize offshore companies for various reasons. These reasons range from offshore business opportunities, estate planning and asset protection, distrust of American laws and society, and threat of persecution. Whatever the reasoning, legitimate offshore planning has nothing to do with secrets or secret accounts. Rather, good offshore planning involves transparent transactions.

To create transparency and establish an effective asset protection and planning tool, a foreign corporation must serve a legitimate business purpose and correctly handle assets located in the United States.

A foreign corporation must have a legitimate purpose[55]. There is no surer way to risk an audit, investigation, and even imprisonment, than to establish a foreign corporation for an improper purpose[56]. (See Infra Tax Cheats & Scammers.)

Individuals must also be careful in using a foreign corporation when the asset they want to protect is located in the United States. If not done correctly, a sale or transfer of a United States based asset will draw the attention and scrutiny of the Internal Revenue Service (IRS). Mostly, the IRS and United States Department of Justice (DOJ) are

---

[55] See Galligan, Ten Important Points to Remember About International Estate Planning, 16-SPG Int'l L. Practicum 53, 61 (2003).

[56] See U.S. v. Beford, 628 F.3d 1232, 1233-34 (Dist. Colo. 2010) (upholding the prison term of an individual who established a foreign corporation for the sole purpose of evading tax payments to the Internal Revenue Service).

concerned about transactions transferring assets or funds with the intent to defraud the government. This is commonly referred to as a "fraudulent transfer."

With this in mind, the soundest way for a foreign entity to possess an asset located in the United States is to have the foreign corporation directly purchase the asset. In this case, the more scrutinized "transfer" is not involved. In addition, where the asset is purchased from a neutral third party, the issue of a fraudulent transfer is completely avoided.

If, on the other hand, a principal of the foreign corporation already owns the asset, it is better to conduct a fully disclosed transfer of the asset than to "manufacture a purchase." If not fully disclosed, the IRS may claim the transfer is fraudulent, pursuant to a "step transaction" theory. In short, a foreign corporation may be a valuable asset protection tool as long as the reason for the entity is legitimate and any United States located assets are properly obtained by the entity.

Who Utilizes Foreign Corporations?

Generally, three types of individuals utilize foreign corporations for asset protection: tax cheats or frauds looking to hide money or assets; individuals who do not intend to violate the law but are unaware of the various disclosure and compliance requirements; fully compliant individuals who establish foreign corporations to legitimately hold funds or assets offshore[57].

---

[57] Kalnins, What Does the U.S. Have Against Foreign Countries?, 24-JUL CBA Rec. 46, 47 (2010).
[58] IRS and Offshore Cheats Plot Next Moves, William P. Barret, Forbes Magazine, October 28, 2009.

Tax Cheats & Scammers

There are individuals and entities who believe they can simply setup an offshore corporation and never pay taxes again. Some of these individuals and entities are well known, and include names like Enron, WorldCom, Igor Olenicoff, and the like. The fact is thousands of businesses engage in offshore tax "cheating" activities or scams. While these individuals and entities may for a short period avoid the IRS and the DOJ, ultimately, they are caught and handed stiff punishments.

Over the past few years, the DOJ has aggressively gone after companies and individuals who attempt to illegally hide assets offshore. The DOJ's most recent attempts include forcing foreign governments and institutions with long standing privacy protections, such as the Switzerland UBS, to disclose account information[58]. While these measures will not catch everyone engaged in illegal or illegitimate offshore activities, the United States Government's far reaching arms have gotten a bit longer.
The increased scrutiny of offshore activities by the DOJ has resulted in several courts reviewing the legitimacy of foreign offshore entities[59].

Again, while individuals may operate an illegitimate foreign corporation for a short period, they will most likely be investigated, prosecuted, and/or convicted of a crime. The risk involved with operating an illegitimate foreign corporation is too great and may result in substantial fines and significant jail time.

---

[58]IRS and Offshore Cheats Plot Next Moves, William P. Barret, Forbes Magazine, October 28, 2009.
[59]See McBreaty v. Vanguard Group, Inc., 353 Fed.Apx. 640 (2nd Cir. 2009); U.S. v. $6,976,934.65, Plus Interset Deposited into Royal Bank of Scotland Intern., Account No. 202956141070, Held in Name of Soulbury Ltd., 554 F.3d 123, 125-26 (DC Cir. 2009); U.S. v. D'Ambrosia, 313 F.3d 987 (7th Cir. 2002); U.S. v. Beford, 628 F.3d 1232, 1233-34 (Dist. Colo. 2010); Terry v. June, 420 F.Supp.2d 493 (W.D. Va. Feb. 27, 2006).

Ignorant Individuals

The second category includes individuals who believe they are establishing foreign entities that are compliant with federal law, but in actuality have failed to follow correct disclosure requirements. For example, the Internal Revenue Service has a myriad of disclosure requirements for offshore planning.

One major disclosure requirement is IRS form TD F 90-22.1. This form requires the signature of an individual who has authority or a "financial interest" in an offshore account or accounts, which have an annual aggregate balance in excess of $10,000. If such an account exists, the individual with signature authority or "financial interest" must disclose the account to the Internal Revenue Service by June 30th of the following year. Failure to do so may result in stiff penalties and criminal prosecution[60].

Many law-abiding individuals who desire to incorporate a foreign entity into their asset protection plan are ignorant of this disclosure. A large number of law-abiding citizens have no idea that such a requirement exists, and that their lives can be turned upside down by failing to comply with this requirement. Unfortunately, ignorance is not a defense and these individuals may face civil and criminal penalties for failing to make the disclosure.

In an effort to encourage individuals to "voluntarily" disclose assets in offshore entities, the IRS decided to give individuals with offshore companies and accounts the opportunity to voluntarily disclose or "come clean" with their accounts. The individuals who utilized this program were able to make proper disclosure without facing any recourse[61]. Regrettably, this program, called the Voluntary Disclosure Program, ended in October 2009.

---

[60]Kalnins, 24-JUL CBA Rec. at 47.
[61]See 26 U.S.C § 7201 (tax evasion); 26 U.S.C. § 7206(1) (filing a false tax return); and 26 U.S.C. § 7203 (failure to file a tax return).

The best way to avoid failing to make proper disclosures is to seek the advice of the Internal Revenue Service, or a competent tax accountant or attorney.

Correctly Established Foreign Entities

While tax evasion is certainly not permitted, tax avoidance and tax deferral opportunities are a different matter. Tax deferral, through the use of an offshore corporation, is complicated and requires several careful considerations. These considerations may include: whether or not the corporation will be considered a controlled foreign corporation (CFC); where the income will be sourced from (i.e., U.S. or a foreign country); what kind of income is involved (Sub-Part F income, PFIC, personal holding company income etc.); whether or not offshore income can be deferred until a distribution is made to repatriate the money to the U.S.

This type of planning is invaluable to individuals who wish to compile profits in a jurisdiction that has a lower tax rate, and defer United States taxation until the funds are distributed to the United States. But, as mentioned above, offshore corporate planning has its own tax and disclosure requirements, ranging from the disclosure of the capitalization and transfer of assets to the corporation (IRS Form 926) to reporting requirements (IRS Form 5471-annual information return), which must be filed each year regardless of income to avoid an annual penalty of $10,000. Many of the same disclosure requirements also exist in the partnership realm.

Proper disclosure is the most important element to consider when incorporating a foreign corporation into an asset protection plan, especially when dealing with an offshore trust. One way to use an offshore trust in an asset protection plan is to establish an offshore "start over" fund consisting of only a portion of an individual's net worth that can be distributed to the individual or their loved ones, pursuant to the fund's estate planning provisions.

Offshore trusts, however, are not for everyone. In deciding whether to establish an offshore trust or foreign corporation, one must weigh: the negative connotation offshore trusts receive by the general uninformed public; or the idea that one is relinquishing title to his or her own assets to a foreign trustee (though through the insertion of a trust protector, one can alleviate much of this concern). Individuals do not realize how much transparency must exist to establish a properly organized and administered offshore trust.

There are also many advantages of using a properly formed foreign corporation and offshore trust. These advantages include the nation's recognition, or lack of foreign judgments; requirements that lawsuits be tried in the foreign nation and pursuant to its laws; favorable statute of fraud provisions or bond posting requirements; and shorter statutes of limitations, among other things.

Regarding disclosure, a properly executed offshore trust and foreign corporation must be extremely transparent, which in turn makes it easier for the IRS and potential creditors to discover. The funding of the trust pursuant to IRS Form 3520, the annual tax return, and the designation of a domestic agent for the purpose of responding to governmental inquiries (as well as disclosure of any account pursuant to IRS Form TD F 90-22.1), means that the United States government and potential creditors know exactly what is in the trust and where the trust is located.

Even though these disclosures are required, the United States government is bound to follow the laws of the country where the corporation is established. Barring a fraudulent conveyance, the foreign trust is completely in opposite of a secret offshore account and does not depend in any way shape or form on nondisclosure or the "hiding" of assets.

Assistance with Offshore Disclosure and Entities

Some individuals and/or entities want assistance with making disclosures. In this case, these individuals may want to obtain the expertise of an "offshore entity manager." An offshore entity manager is a public or private company that will assist you in maintaining your offshore entity in the country in which your entity is established. Because disclosure laws are extremely difficult to understand and follow, an offshore entity manager will assist you in legally moving assets from the United States.

Another strategy to protect your assets is to use a domestic leasing company. The function of a leasing company allows you to remove business assets, especially valuable equipment, from the risks associated with the business.

For example, if the assets you use are owned by a third party company who leases them to you, they become an obligation and not an asset, of which may be under attack. In that case, not only would the asset be safe, but also the payment of the lease is contractual and could be transferred to a creditor who gains control.

What is the Role of a Foreign Charging Order (COPEs) When Utilizing a Foreign Entity in an Asset Protection Plan?

Most foreign partnership and LLC statutes provide for charging orders. As mentioned above, a foreign entity is typically used in asset protection plans, in conjunction with a foreign trust. The benefit of using a foreign trust is that the income earned by the trust will be taxable to the estate owner, and on death of the trust, assets will be included in the grantor's estate[62]. Furthermore, a foreign trust with a foreign trustee, makes it more difficult for creditors to pierce or enforce a charging order against the foreign entity[63]. The success of the device, however, depends to a large extent on the law of the foreign jurisdiction and the attitude of the foreign courts. Other factors that may affect the success of a foreign entity or trust include the extent to which the underlying assets remains in the United States and the ability of the estate owners' creditor to find a way to reach them. If not careful, foreign trusts may not accomplish their intended goal.

One solution might be avoiding a foreign corporation altogether and using a domestic trust. For example, several states, such as Alaska and Delaware, have created vehicles to afford individuals greater protection. For Instance, Delaware law now permits any individual to establish a discretionary "self-settled" trust, where the donor is permitted to be a beneficiary. If structured correctly, the assets contained in the trusts will are not subject to the claims of the donor's creditors. As a general proposition, the Delaware asset protection trust is designed to hold cash, securities, and other non-real property assets[64].

---

[62]See IRS Reg. § 25.2511-2(c).

[63]See Weinstock & Neumann, Planning an Estate: A Guidebook of Principles and Techniques, ch. 12.74 (2010).

[64]See Henkel, Estate Planning and Wealth Preservation: Strategies and Solutions, Paragraph 53.04[1][c]; Osborne & Schurig, Asset Protection: Domestic and International Law and Tactics, ch. 14A.

Offshore opportunities greatly differ from domestic entities. Individuals should not limit their business and asset protection options for fear of the appearance of being a "tax evader." With the existing disclosure laws, accessibility of international travel, and the Internet, foreign borders are much more accessible than they have ever been. In fact, the protections and benefits of foreign markets are available for all those who legitimately desire to utilize them. Whether that consists of establishing a holding company in Luxembourg or organizing a Chinese corporation, the opportunity is available in our ever-changing global economy. The key is that the right circumstances must exist and the individual or entity must be willing to comply firmly with United States disclosure laws[65].

---

[65]Kalnins, 24-JUL CBA Rec. at 47.

Chapter **17**

Aggressive Asset Protection Strategies

Should I Incorporate Aggressive Asset Protection Strategies Into My Plan?

Aggressive asset protection strategies vary in type, manner, and method. Aggressive strategies include utilization of a foreign corporation; implementation of a foreign trust; establishment of offshore accounts; and funding of specialized trusts. While these strategies are available options, whether or not an individual desires to incorporate them depends upon that person's circumstances and in some cases, tolerance to risk. One risk an individual with an aggressive strategy may face is the increased likelihood that the government will attack the plan[66].

As preached throughout this book, the key is transparency and disclosure. If a plan is not set up correctly, an individual may face prosecution for tax evasion (26 U.S.C § 7201), filing a false tax return (26 U.S.C. § 7206(1)), and/or failing to file a tax return (26 U.S.C. § 7203).

---

[66]Turner, Irrevocable Trusts, IRREVTR § 35:5.

Of course, aggressive asset protection plans are not only used to reduce tax liability. They are also used to protect assets from judgments and creditors. One aggressive approach to take is to try to intimidate your creditors in an attempt to make them go away. Experience shows, however, that though this type of approach may work for the short term, it never fully succeeds. If anything, a hostile approach agitates creditors into more aggressively seeking after the asset.

A better approach is to be straightforward and direct without being rude or hostile. Nine times out of ten, a calm, quiet, and collected response will have better results than an "in your face" strategy. A person who has properly set up an estate plan or asset protection plan has little to fear. Anger and/or agitation will only escalate the situation; stay calm and relaxed.

What Type of Aggressive Strategies May I Use Without Drawing Too Much Attention to My Plan?

Again, the main area of concern is fraudulent transfers. There are several legitimate strategies that an individual may employ to protect his or her assets. Such strategies include legal entities; spendthrift trusts; qualified terminable interest property trusts; self-settled offshore asset protection trusts; Alaska trusts; Delaware qualified disposition trusts; and Nevada spendthrift trusts.

Legal Entities

Numerous categories of asset protection instruments have been available for decades[67]. Some of the traditional methods of asset protection include the use of limited liability corporations (LLC), limited liability partnerships (LLP), and family limited partnerships (FLP).

The use of LLCs, LLPs, and FLPs as asset protection instruments originated for legitimate businesses purposes, with the added benefit of protection from personal liability from the creditors of the business. As such, these asset protection instruments have the distinction of serving a legitimate purpose; accordingly, they have been honored, and continue to be honored. For that reason, LLCs, LLPs, and FLPs are available as legitimate asset protection instruments if the entity is properly established and administered[68].

When an asset is correctly purchased or transferred to an LLC, LLP, or FLP, a creditor will have to rely on a charging order to attempt to attain relief. LLCs, LLPs, and FLPs created in states such as Alaska, Nevada, or Wyoming, which have favorable charging orders will make it especially difficult for a creditor to pierce the corporate veil and take the asset[69].

Revocable Living Trusts With Spendthrift Provisions

Another legitimate tool is a revocable living trust. The claim that a revocable living trust does not provide asset protection is not true. For example, under a proper A-B trust system, once a spouse dies, the trust assets obtain substantial asset protection. In particular, a well-drafted trust limits the beneficiaries from encumbering the trust assets.

---

[67]See Nichols, Note, "I See the Sword of Damocles Is Hanging Above Your Head!" Domestic Venue Asset Protection Trusts, Credit Due Judgments, and Conflict of Law Disputes, 22 Rev. Litig. 473, 478 (2003).

[68]See Claudia R. Tobler & Ingrid Michelsen Hillinger, Asset Protection Devices: Twyne's Case Re-Told, 9 J. Bankr. L. & Prac. 3, 4, 17-18 (1999).

[69]Turner, Revocable Trusts 5th edition, ch. 64 (2010).

Furthermore, when the trust contains a spendthrift provision, it stops creditors from obtaining an interest in the trust assets.

Qualified Terminable Interest Property Trusts (QTIP)

One legal way to transfer a large estate and/or asset is to use a decedent's trust, also called a credit bypass trust in conjunction with a qualified terminable interest property trust (QTIP). This approach avoids adverse tax consequences, assuming the spouses have an equal ownership in all trust assets and the combined value of the decedent's trust and the QTIP are equal to fifty percent (50%) of the total estate. The remaining fifty percent (50%) would be allocated to the survivor's trust. Under these circumstances, the QTIP would have the same asset protection benefits as had been suggested for the decedent's trust.

Self-Settled Offshore Asset Protection Trusts (OAPTs)

As previously discussed, some individuals seek asset protection via self-settled Offshore Asset Protection Trusts (OAPT). "[B]y 1994 it was estimated that over $1 trillion were invested in OAPTs[70]." The primary purpose of these offshore trusts is to shield assets from potential future creditors.

Self-settled OAPTs have been available for decades. In certain cases, OAPTs are more favored than LLCs, LLPs, and FLPs because of the added layers of protection they provide. This is a perfectly viable option, but is very aggressive, and individuals who choose to implement this strategy may have to be willing to suffer contempt charges in exchange for keeping their assets protected.

---

[70]See Roder, Note, American Asset Protection Trusts: Alaska and Delaware Move "Offshore" Trusts onto the Mainland, 49 Syracuse L. Rev. 1253, 1265.

One of these layers of protection is the existence or lack of international treaties[71]. For example, if an international treaty or agreement does not exist between the United States and an offshore jurisdiction, it becomes extremely difficult to force repatriation of the assets. As a result, while a creditor may be able to obtain a judgment in an American court, the creditor will not be able to enforce the judgment in a foreign jurisdiction that does not have a treaty or agreement with the United States.

Having an OAPT in a jurisdiction with a "debtor friendly" legal system adds another layer of protection. These features tend to make the offshore trust more attractive to those seeking ways to protect their assets than the domestic LLCs, LLPs, and FLPs.

Offshore trusts, however, do not solve all asset protection problems. In most cases, the settlor[72] of the trust is not familiar with foreign procedures or the offshore manager selected to administer the trust. Because of the nature of the offshore trust business, a settlor does not know the individual or entity employed to administer the trust. The settlor takes a huge risk in handing over the assets of the trust to an unknown individual or entity.

One might be tempted to establish an OAPT where the settlor is also the trustee. Because the Settlor retains control of the assets, he or she is not afforded the same protections as an OAPT with a foreign trustee. In FTC v. Affordable Media, LLC[73], the court held it had jurisdiction over defendants who had appointed themselves as co-trustees of their own OAPT for which they also acted as settlors. The defendants (the Andersons) were involved in a Ponzi scheme that resulted in their

---

[71] See Marty-Nelson, Taxing Offshore Asset Protection Trusts: Icing on the Cake?, 15 Va. Tax Rev. 399, 400-01 (1996).

[72] A settlor is the individual who donates the asset to the trust. In many cases that is the individual who is seeking to protect his/her assets.

[72] A settlor is the individual who donates the asset to the trust. In many cases that is the individual who is seeking to protect his/her assets.

[73] 179 F.3d 1228 (9th Cir. 1999).

investors losing all of their money while the defendants transferred the commissions of their ill-gotten gains to an OAPT in the Cook Islands[74].

After the district court entered a preliminary injunction against them, the Andersons argued they did not have control over the OAPT because their appointed trustee in the Cook Islands had invoked an "event of duress" clause, which automatically removed the Andersons as co-trustees[75]. Looking at the level of control the Andersons retained over the trust, the court upheld the contempt order[76]. Ultimately, it was the fact that the Andersons named themselves as co-trustees, which allowed the court to hold that they were in contempt for not forcing the Cook Island trustee to return the wrongfully obtained funds to the United States[77]. Had the Andersons known the trustee personally, they might have been more willing to name them as the sole trustee of the OAPT. With only a foreign trustee, they would have lacked the requisite control for the court to find them in contempt.

OAPTs are legitimate asset protection tools. However, while there are definite advantages to OAPTs one must be willing to take certain risks, such as appointing a foreign trustee.

---

[74]Id. at 1231-32.
[75]Id. at 1242.
[76]Id.
[77]Id.

Alaska Trusts

In 1997, the State of Alaska enacted the Alaska Trust Act (ATA)[78]. The current version of the ATA provides an Alaska trust which has a spendthrift provision that prevents a subsequent creditor from satisfying a judgment against a beneficiary of the trust, unless the settlor is the beneficiary and the creditor was a creditor of the settlor at the time the trust was created[79]. Thus, an Alaska trust with a spendthrift provision offers creditors very little opportunity to collect from the assets in the trust.

Alaskan laws are extremely debtor friendly, and limit the creditor from accessing assets in the trust, unless the debtor, acting as settlor of the trust made a fraudulent transfer; limited the ability to revoke or terminate the trust; or required the trust's income or principal to be distributed to the settlor[80].

There are some limitations to Alaska trusts. In order to establish an Alaska trust, some or all of the settlor's property must be physically located in the State of Alaska[81]. The statute also reserves exclusive jurisdiction over Alaska trusts in Alaska courts. As a result, the state laws of Alaska govern validity, construction, and administration of Alaska trusts.

These restrictions are not arbitrary and provide a benefit to the trustee. For example, having Alaska law govern the trust makes it easier for the trustee to manage, because the trustee only has to worry about the laws of Alaska when determining his or her duties and obligations. Furthermore, requiring the property to be physically located in Alaska protects the debtor from the risk that another jurisdiction will not honor the trust or place the same restrictions on creditors as Alaska does.

---

[78] 1997 Alaska Sess. Laws 006.
[79] Alaska Stat. § 34.40.110(b) (2008).
[80] Id.
[81] Alaska Stat. § 13.36.035(a), (c) (2008).

The ATA also contains restrictive provisions that prevent creditors from challenging a trust. For example, Alaska Statute 13.36.310 states that unless there is a violation under section 34.40.110, a trust that otherwise falls under laws of Alaska is not void, voidable, liable to be set aside, defective in any fashion, or questionable as to the [donor's] capacity, . . . on the grounds that the trust . . . defeats a right, claim, or interest conferred by law on a person by reason of a personal or business relationship with the [donor] . . . or by way of a marital or similar right.

This protection allows a trust to withstand a creditors attack unless a conveyance is made with the intent to hinder, delay, or defraud; the donor retains the power to revoke or terminate the trust without the consent of persons with substantial interests; all the income or principal will be paid to the settlor; or the settlor is in default by thirty (30) days or more in child support payments pursuant to a court order[82]. To challenge the validity of the trust, creditors must overcome a great burden.

The ATA allows an individual or entity to retain possession of a testamentary non-general power of appointment and still protect the trust property from creditors. The protection of the trust's assets, however, does not limit liability of assets from an estate tax perspective. Usually, a person who holds a general power of appointment will be subject to taxation under Internal Revenue Code § 2041, whether or not the power is actually exercised, because mere possession of a general power of appointment is an interest in property. For estate tax purposes, the right to decide who will enjoy the beneficial interest in property is enough of a property interest to require inclusion in the gross estate of the power holder[83].

Consequently, if an Alaska trust settlor retains a testamentary non-general power of appointment in the trust property, the settlor retains

---

[82]Alaska Stat. 34.40.110(b).
[83]I.R.C. § 2033.

some control of the trust property. In that case, the property subject to such power should continue to be treated as a property interest of the settlor. Internal Revenue Code § 2041, however, does not specifically address the consequences of a settlor's retention of a non-general power of appointment. Thus, it is unknown what effect the control will have other than the consequence that the property will be taxed to the settlor.

The special power of appointment contemplated by the Internal Revenue Code was intended to be bestowed upon a third party by the settlor. It was not intended to be a power that the settlor granted to him or herself. Therefore, by definition, the special power retained by the donor in accordance with the authority granted by the ATA should not be treated as a special power deserving special tax treatment under the code.

When the power is created by the settlor and vested in him or herself, the fact remains that the settlor retains control. Regardless of gift tax consequences, the donor retains a property interest over the trust property after the transfer. As such, possession of such a power by the settlor should cause the asset to be included, for tax purposes, in the donor's gross estate. One exemption to this rule is if the settlor releases his or her non-general power of appointment over the property while on his or her deathbed. Under those circumstances, the estate would not be required to include the asset within the gross estate, and would not be subject to the three year look-back period under Internal Revenue Code § 2035.

Delaware Qualified Dispositions in Trust Act (QDTA)

Delaware enacted the QDTA in July 1997, a few months after Alaska enacted the ATA[84]. Like the ATA, the Delaware QDTA provides considerable protection to trusts that contain a spendthrift provision. Furthermore, the Delaware QDTA also permits the settlor to retain the power of appointment, and requires Delaware law to control challenges as to the "validity, construction, and administration of the trust[85]."

The Delaware QDTA also has some statutory provisions which are excluded from the ATA. First, Section 3573 provides limitations on qualified dispositions with respect to certain specified creditors. A "qualified disposition" is a "disposition by or from a transferor to a qualified trustee or qualified trustees, with or without consideration, by means of a trust instrument[86]." Therefore, the Delaware QDTA creates a special category of creditors who may be authorized to make a valid claim against the trust. With that said, the circumstances under which these creditors may make a valid claim is extremely limited.

One of the limited exceptions for creditor access is based on whether there is a court order for child support or alimony. A settlor cannot use a Delaware QDTA to avoid paying child support or alimony[87]. Another exception allows a creditor to pierce the trust to obtain payment for "death, personal injury, or property damage" caused by the settlor's action or inaction[88]. Thus, a Delaware QDTA opens greater exposure than the ATA, which does not have an exception for personal injury cases.

---

[84]Del. Code Ann.tit.12 § 3570(10) (2007).
[85]Id. at § 3570(11)(a); Alaska Stat. § 13.36.035(c).
[86]Del. Code Ann.tit.12 § 3570(7) (2007).
[87]Del. Code Ann. tit. 12, § 3573(1).
[88]Del. Code Ann. tit. 12, § 3573(3).

Nevada Spendthrift Trust Act (STA)

In 1999, Nevada amended its laws to provide for self-settled spendthrift trusts. As with the ATA and Delaware's QDTA, the Nevada STA trust provides protection from creditors while leaving a certain level of control and benefit to the settlor. To create the self-settled trust in accordance with Nevada's STA, the trust must meet the following requirements: irrevocability; no requirement to make distributions of any part of the income or principal to the settlor; and, no intention to "hinder, delay, or defraud known creditors[89]."

The Nevada STA is consistent with the ATA and the Delaware QDTA. One exception is that if nothing is specifically mentioned in the trust, the discretionary provision of the trust governs. The statute is also designed to provide extra protection to settlors against creditor claims and cover the key provisions under the Internal Revenue Code for favorable transfer tax treatment.

---

[89]Nev. Rev. Stat. Ann. § 166.010 (2009).

Glossary

Annual Exclusion
The amount that any person may give away in each calendar year without incurring gift tax. Not all gifts will qualify for the annual exclusion. Only outright gifts or gifts of a present interest made to certain types of trusts will qualify.

Annuitant
The person whose lifespan is used for making income payments. The owner of the annuity policy will determine whose life will be used as the measuring life and in many cases the owner and the annuitant will be the same.

Annuitize
The process of converting the balance in a deferred annuity contract into a stream of payments for a period of years or for someone's lifetime.

Annuity
A tax-deferred contract with an insurance company or other entity that provides for the payment of income for a predetermined amount of time, such as a person's lifetime or a certain number of years. See also deferred annuity and immediate annuity.

Asset Protection and Asset Protection Planning
The process of structuring one's estate to obtain more advantageous creditor protection from future lawsuits and claims. Different types of asset protection solutions are available depending on the size of estate and the desire to obtain the best possible asset protection solutions.

Asset Protection Trusts (APT)
Trusts designed to hold assets in a creditor protected entity. Asset protection trusts are most protective and effective when created as

offshore trusts, as they are typically out of the reach of US courts. Currently eleven states have enacted onshore asset protection trust legislation. However, this legislation has never been tested or endorsed by a US court. As such, it is currently unknown whether onshore or domestic asset protection trusts will be a successful asset protection solution.

Beneficiary

Depending on the context, a beneficiary will be a person or entity named in : (i) a trust who receives real or personal property in accordance with the terms contained in the trust agreement or declaration of trust; or (ii) an annuity who receives money remaining in the annuity upon the death of the owner or annuitant.

Charging Order

A court-authorized right granted to a judgment creditor to attach distributions made from a business entity, such as a limited partnership (LP) or limited liability company (LLC), or to a debtor who is a partner of the business entity.

Charging Order Protected Entity (COPE)

Charging Order Protected Entity (COPE) is the term used to describe entities for which external creditors are usually limited to the charging order remedy.

Charitable Lead Annuity Trust (CLAT)

A split interest trust with a charitable beneficiary that has the right to receive a series of annual payments in the form of an annuity amount each year for a predetermined or stated term. A family member or non-charitable beneficiary has the right to receive the remaining trust assets when the trust term expires. The annuity amount payable to the charity is calculated on the initial value of the trust assets at the time the trust is created.

Charitable Lead Trust (CLT)

A split interest trust where the charity receives income and the non-charitable beneficiary receives everything that is left (i.e. the remainder of the trust) after the charitable payments have been made for the required term. Charitable lead trusts are frequently used with stock, in closely held or family business with low basis to help achieve both tax and charitable planning goals.

Charitable Lead Unitrust Trust (CLUT)

A trust where the charitable beneficiary has the right to receive a unitrust or annuity payment each year for a specified term. The annuity amount is calculated based upon the value of the trust assets at the beginning of each year of the trust. After the stated term, the remaining trust balance will be distributed to the designated family member or to the non-charitable beneficiary.

Charitable Remainder Annuity Trust (CRAT)

A trust wherein a family member or non-charitable beneficiary has the right to receive the annuity payment each year during a stated term of years or for the beneficiary's lifetime. The annuity amount will be calculated on the initial value of the trust assets when the trust is created. After the stated term or the beneficiary's death, the remainder of the trust will be distributed to the charitable beneficiary.

Charitable Remainder Trust (CRT)

A trust where a family member or non-charitable beneficiary receives a stream of payments and the charitable beneficiary receives the balance or remainder of the trust. This is often used to achieve both charitable, estate and income tax goals with low-basis stock holdings while providing income payments to the grantor.

Charitable Remainder Unitrust Trust (CRUT)

A trust where the non-charitable beneficiary has the right to receive a unitrust or annuity amount each year during the specified term or for the beneficiary's lifetime. The annuity amount is calculated based on the value of the trust assets at the beginning of each year of the trust. After passage of the stated term or upon the beneficiary's death, the remainder of the trust is distributed to the charitable beneficiary.

Corporation

The most common form of business organization, and one which is chartered by a state, and given many legal rights as an entity separate from its owners. This form of business is characterized by the limited liability of its owners, the issuance of shares of easily transferable stock, and existence as a going concern. The process of becoming a corporation, called incorporating, gives the company separate legal standing from its owners and protects those owners from being personally liable in the event that the company is sued (a condition known as limited liability). Incorporation also provides companies with a more flexible way to manage their ownership structure. In addition, there are different tax implications for corporations, although these can be both advantageous and disadvantageous. In these respects, corporations differ from sole proprietorships and limited partnerships.

Deferred Annuity

A type of annuity or retirement account issued by an insurance company that is intended to provide tax-deferred growth on the accumulated income. This type of product may have good asset protection qualities depending on state laws.

Disclaimer

No one can force you to accept an inheritance, and when you elect to turn down or refuse an inheritance it is called a disclaimer. Disclaimers are usually in the form of a written document and can be used to accept some, but not all of an inheritance. In order for a disclaimer to be qualified under the Internal Revenue Code as a non-taxable transfer, the disclaimer must be made within nine months after the date of the death or transfer. It must be made in compliance with state laws, and no income or benefits may have been received by the person disclaiming.

Domestic Asset Protection Trust
A self-settled spendthrift trust drafted under the laws of one of the ten states that have abolished the rule against self-settled spendthrift trusts, thereby permitting grantors to create their own asset protection trust. The eleven states that now permit onshore asset protection trusts include Alaska, Delaware, Missouri, Nevada, Oklahoma, Rhode Island, South Dakota, Tennessee, Utah and Wyoming. No significant cases exist that have endorsed the use of onshore or domestic asset protection trusts as a viable asset protection planning solution.

Domestic Trustee
An asset protection term used to describe one or more of the trustees of the asset protection trust. The domestic trustee may be an individual or corporate fiduciary and may serve alone or in conjunction with a foreign trustee, depending on how the asset protection trust is designed.

Estate Tax
A transfer tax imposed on transfers occurring at the decedent's death. The estate tax in 2009 is 45% on all assets in excess of the $3,500,000 applicable exemption amount. Each decedent has an exemption from estate taxes that was previously referred to as the unified credit exemption of $3,500,000. The amount that can be passed at death, free from estate tax is reduced by any lifetime gifts, unless an exclusion or exemption is used to exempt otherwise taxable gifts made during the person's lifetime. In 2011, estates in excess of $1,000,000 will be taxed at 55%.

Equity Indexed Annuity
A special type of tax-deferred annuity that guarantees a return based on a stated percentage of a predetermined index such as the S & P 500 Index.

Family Limited Partnership (FLP)

An asset protection planning solution that is most effective when the limited partnership interests are owned by a domestic or foreign asset protection trust instead of an individual or estate planning trust. The partnership interests are typically owned by family members instead of business partners. See limited partnership.

Foreign Trust

A designation that refers either to an offshore asset protection trust, a trust with one or more foreign trustee or a trust which, pursuant to IRC §7701, is not classified as a domestic trust for income tax purposes.

Generation Skipping Transfer Tax

A transfer tax imposed at a rate equal to the highest estate tax rate on gifts or estate transfers where the transferred assets pass, or will pass, to recipients two or more generations below the donor, without being subject to the imposition of estate tax at the intervening generations. Each donor has an exemption that may be used to offset the GST tax.

Generation Skipping Trust

An inter vivos trust or testamentary trust designed to exist for more than one generation into the future and qualify for the generation skipping transfer tax exemption, while avoiding inclusion in the estates of the beneficiaries for estate tax purposes.

Gift Tax

A transfer tax imposed on transfers made by a donor during their lifetime that are in excess of the federal applicable exemption amount of $1,000,000, which amount is not indexed for inflation or scheduled to increase. In the event that the gift tax exemption is not fully used during a person's lifetime, the unused exemption will exempt transfers made at death from the federal estate tax. Any person may make an unlimited number of annual exclusion gifts each year without incurring a gift tax liability.

Gift Trust or Gifting Trust
A trust designed to hold gifted or inherited assets for the benefit of individuals or charities. It is typically created for beneficiaries who are unable to manage gifted assets, obtain asset protection, or minimize gift, estate, and generation skipping transfer taxes to the grantor and the beneficiaries.

Grantor
The person or entity that transfers real or personal property in trust to a trustee or co-trustees under written or oral directions to the trustee. The trustee may be instructed to hold, manage, invest, account for, and distribute the property to those specified as a trust beneficiary in accordance with the terms set forth in the trust instrument.

Grantor Retained Annuity Trust (GRAT)
An irrevocable inter vivos trust under which a grantor transfers his or her interest in real or personal property to a trustee they have selected to hold these assets for the specified term or duration of the trust. During each year of the term, the grantor receives an annuity amount based upon the value of the assets at the creation of the trust. Upon expiration of the term, the trust property passes to the remainder beneficiary or beneficiaries. It is primarily used to gift property to the remainder beneficiary that is susceptible to application of valuation discounts and actuarial discounts. These discounts are based on the grantor's age and the term of the trust, and are most beneficial if the property is expected to appreciate in value.

Grantor Retained Unitrust Trust (GRUT)
A GRUT is an irrevocable inter vivos grantor trust under which a grantor transfers their interest in real or personal property to a trustee whom they select to hold some of their assets during a specified trust term. The grantor will receive an annuity payment based on the value of the assets at the beginning of the year for each year the trust is in existence. When the trust term expires, the trust property passes to the remainder beneficiaries. This technique is primarily used for gifting purposes to efficiently transfer family wealth to a remainder beneficiary by taking advantage of valuation and actuarial discounts

based on the grantor's age and the term of the trust The discounts are most advantageous when the property is expected to significantly appreciate in value.

Immediate Annuity
An annuity that is purchased with a lump sum and that is required to return payments to its owner within a time frame no longer than twelve months. Immediate annuities may be fixed or variable depending on the terms and investments.

International Business Company (IBC)
Corporation formed under the corporate legislation of a tax haven (such as Bahamas, Panama, Turks & Caicos). IBC's are not usually authorized to do business in the country of formation (incorporation) but can have offices that manage global operations. In addition to the usual benefits accruing from incorporation (such as limited liability), IBCs also enjoy banking and corporate secrecy, rapid formation, low cost, little or no taxation, and minimal filing and reporting requirements. Some tax havens also allow nominee shareholders and directors.

Intentionally Defective Grantor Trust (IDGT)
An IDGT is an irrevocable inter vivos trust created by a grantor for the benefit of beneficiaries (other than the grantor). It has the unique treatment under the Internal Revenue Code of having all of the income taxed to the grantor instead of the beneficiaries. IDGTs are typically used to assist the grantor in making gifts to his or her descendants in order to exclude the property from the grantor's taxable estate for estate tax purposes. Since the grantor is legally responsible for paying the tax on the income earned by the trust, the grantor's estate tax savings are enhanced. Additionally, the trust assets are increased, since the trust isn't reduced by the amount of income tax that otherwise would have been paid from the trust. This technique is frequently used in conjunction with a sale of discounted assets by the grantor to the trust, with the effect of avoiding capital gains on the sale of the assets.

Inter Vivos Trust

A trust created during the grantor's lifetime, usually by means of a written trust instrument or agreement. A trust created after the death of the grantor is referred to as a testamentary trust.

Irrevocable Trust

A trust that cannot, by its terms, be amended or revoked by the grantor. Irrevocable trusts can be created during a grantor's lifetime for asset protection purposes, for life insurance or for completed gifting trusts, generation skipping trusts, qualified personal residence trusts (QPRT), grantor retained annuity trusts (GRAT), intentionally defective grantor trusts (IDGT), charitable remainder trusts, or charitable lead trusts. Some common types of irrevocable trusts which are created at the death of the grantor as testamentary trusts include applicable exemption or unified credit trusts; charitable remainder or charitable lead trusts, created under another trust agreement; or generation skipping trusts, which are frequently designed as asset protection trusts for current and future family members.

Judgment

A decision by a court that describes the rights and obligations of both parties in a lawsuit. In small claims court, for example, a judgment might be entered against a customer who owes money to your business. The judgment may be that the person must pay what he or she owes, or some part of what is owed.

Life Insurance Trust (LIT)

An irrevocable life insurance trust is a trust that is intended to hold primarily life insurance policies on the life of the grantor or, on occasion, a policy on the joint lives of the grantor and the grantor's spouse. The major estate planning advantage is to remove the death benefit from the grantor's taxable estate for estate tax purposes. The major asset protection purpose is to use the irrevocable trust to provide a creditor protected entity for the spouse or children. Insurance trusts need to be carefully designed to qualify for annual exclusion gifts, as typically gifts made in trust won't qualify as transfers of a present interest. Therefore, absent proper planning, a gift tax would arise when the insurance premiums are paid. Many insurance trusts are designed as asset protection trusts, beneficiary controlled trusts, or dynasty trusts. These trusts would all contain provisions for continuing testamentary trusts after the grantor's death for the grantor's spouse, children, grandchildren, and other family or charitable beneficiaries.

Limited Liability Company (LLC)
A business or asset protection planning technique that helps to protect the owner from lawsuits originating against the LLC. Different states have different laws that significantly affect the ability to protect the owner's personal assets. LLCs are most effective when used in conjunction with a domestic or foreign asset protection trust and when the LLCs are created in a state that, by statute, limits the remedies to charging orders of protection only.

Limited Partnership (LP)
A limited partnership is a partnership created under the limited partnership laws of a particular state. A limited partnership has a general partner, who has unlimited liability for operation of the partnership, and limited partners who are not subject to the claims of creditors of the partnership. Limited partnerships are used in conjunction with many asset protection trusts. Limited partners do not participate in the management of the partnership. General partners have the ability to manage the operations of the partnership, as well as to determine when and if any distributions will be made to the limited partners. Most partnership agreements restrict a limited partner from transferring their partnership interest. From an asset protection perspective, a limited partnership as a standalone solution is not very effective. When used in conjunction with an asset protection trust, the limited partnership offers a higher degree of protection.

Marital Deduction
The marital deduction is an unlimited deduction against estate tax and gift tax for transfers made by a married person to their spouse during their life or at death. The transfers can either be made outright or in qualifying trusts created specifically to protect the unlimited marital deduction. This is primarily a technique to avoid the loss of an estate

on the death of the first spouse by deferring estate taxes until the death of the surviving spouse, thereby ensuring that 100% of the estate is available for the survivor.

Marital Deduction Trust
A trust that is designed to qualify for the unlimited marital deduction for estate and gift tax purposes. Several types of trusts can qualify for the unlimited marital deduction, including: general power of appointment marital trusts, qualified terminable interest property trusts, and qualified domestic trusts which are used if the surviving spouse is not a citizen of the US.

Non-Qualified Annuity
An annuity that is tax deferred and purchased by its owner with after-tax dollars instead of in a tax-qualified retirement plan like an IRA.

Not-for-Profit Corporation or Non-Profit Corporation
A corporation created under applicable state law to be exempt from income taxes. A not-for-profit corporation is typically a charitable entity created for educational, religious, scientific, or artistic purposes. The operation of which is required to be in accordance with applicable state and tax laws.

Offshore Asset Protection Trust
A trust created with one of the objectives being to obtain creditor protection from future lawsuits and to preserve accumulated wealth from future litigation claims. Offshore asset protection trusts are created under the law of countries with legislation that is more protective than the laws of the United States and may have both US trustees and foreign trustees. Offshore asset protection trusts are viewed by most knowledgeable planners as offering the highest level of creditor protection possible.

Personal Representative (Executor)

A person or entity named in a last will and testament and/or appointed by the probate court. The appointed person is responsible for collecting the decedent's assets, paying the decedent's debts, taxes and expenses. The executor is also responsible for selling assets of the estate and distributing the remaining property and money according to the terms of the will, or in accordance with the laws of intestate succession of the state of residence. The personal representative is a court-appointed fiduciary with great responsibilities such as preserving and protecting the estate assets, accounting to the heirs and estate beneficiaries for all income and expenses, and filing all required personal, federal, and state estate tax returns for the decedent and the estate.

Postnuptial Agreement

A contract agreed to by both spouses after their marriage, that defines each spouse's rights to their marital, non-marital, community and jointly-owned property in the event of divorce, legal separation or the death of one of the parties. A postnuptial contract is considered to be valid and enforceable if it complies with the statutory requirements for pre-nuptial agreements. This is a first level asset protection planning technique for anyone with significant assets who remarried without having sought the advice of a legal advisor prior to their remarriage. Although the use of postnuptial agreements is not as common as pre-marital agreements, they do provide some protection if both parties are willing to agree to the terms and waive some of their marital rights after the fact. Pre-nuptial agreements are normally viewed to be a better asset protection solution as the terms are voluntarily agreed to prior to the marriage.

Pre-Nuptial Agreement

A Contract entered into by an engaged couple prior to their marriage which sets forth their respective rights in marital, non-marital, community, and jointly-owned property in the event of divorce, legal separation, or the death of one of the parties. In order for pre-nuptial agreements to be enforceable, most states require that: (i) there be a full and fair disclosure of the earnings and property of each party; (ii) the parties have had an adequate time to review the agreement prior to the wedding; (iii) each party had the opportunity to consult with legal counsel of their own choice; and (iv) the agreement be in writing, executed and acknowledged by the parties in the presence of witnesses and a notary public.

Private Foundation

A trust or not-for-profit corporation that provides for distributions only to charities during its term. Foundations may be structured as a perpetual trust or as a corporation. The governing body would be either a board of trustees or a board of directors.

Probate

The legal process of re-titling wealth from the name of the decedent to its new owner. Probate is required whenever the size of the estate is greater than the statutory amount, which is typically $50,000 to $100,000. The probate judge determines if the decedent's will is valid and appoints the personal representative or executor to collect the decedent's assets, pay the outstanding debts, and transfer the remaining assets to the decedent's trust or named heirs.

Probate Estate

Probate assets only include assets that are payable to the estate or are held in the sole name of the decedent at the time of death. Since a deceased person can no longer own assets, the probate court needs to determine who the new owner of each asset will be. Probate provides virtually no asset protection since notice to all creditors is required and each creditor has months in which to file a claim against the estate. Property held in more than one name such as joint tenancy with rights of survivorship, or community property with rights of survivorship are not included in the decedent's probate estate and will pass to the surviving owner. In addition, if a proper beneficiary designation was made for proceeds of life insurance, annuities, IRAs or qualified retirement benefits, they will not normally be included in the decedent's estate unless the beneficiary designation specifically designates the decedent's estate or was not properly made.

Qualified Annuity
An annuity that is purchased with pre-tax dollars in a tax-deferred and qualified retirement plan such as an IRA account.

Qualified Personal Residence Trust (QPRT)
An inter vivos or living trust where the grantor transfers their interest in a personal residence to the trustee to hold for the grantor's use and occupation for the specified term of the trust. At the termination of the trust term, the residence passes to the remainder beneficiaries. This technique is typically used to make gifts of a vacation or second home to the grantor's children or grandchildren. QPRTs receive advantageous valuation discounts, as well as actuarial discounts based on the grantor's age and the term of the trust, and when a home that is appreciating in value is put into the QPRT, the best benefits are received.

Revocable Trust
An inter vivos or living trust that is designed to be amended or revoked by the grantor or settler. This is the type of trust used for estate planning purposes to avoid probate, and has no asset protection qualities for the grantor. Properly drafted revocable living trusts (RLTs) typically contain lifetime provisions for the care of the grantor, the grantor's spouse and children, as well as provisions for taking care of the grantor upon the grantor's disability and death. RLTs should also contain dispositive terms that govern the amount and timing of the distribution of the grantor's assets after their death.

Settlor
The person who settled or created a trust. Also referred to as the grantor.

Split Interest
A gift or transfer which will be divided into a charitable share and non-charitable share. Some common examples of split interest trusts would be a charitable remainder trust or a charitable lead trust.

Tax Deferred

A type of investment that is not subject to current income taxation. This is typically an insurance product such as an annuity or a retirement solution such as an IRA. Income is accumulated and all income taxes are deferred until withdrawals are made.

Tax Free Exchange

IRC § 1031 and 1035 govern tax-deferred exchanges of real estate and insurance products. These sections permit a taxpayer to exchange property, insurance policies, or annuities for other similar property without having to pay a gain on the income or increase in value. From an asset protection standpoint, §1035 permits an individual to exchange a policy with a large cash value with a new policy that may have better asset protection features, including Swiss annuities or foreign life insurance.

Testamentary Trust

A trust created after the grantor's death in accordance with the terms stated in a last will or testament or in accordance with the provisions of another revocable trust agreement.

Trust

A legal arrangement under which the grantor or settlor transfers their assets, including real and personal property, investments, and business interests to a trustee or trustees. Specific oral or preferably written directions are given to the trustee as to how the trust assets should be held, managed, invested, accounted for, and distributed to the beneficiaries on the terms set forth in the trust instrument. Trusts may be created for asset protection purposes, estate planning purposes, or simply to govern the lifetime management and distribution of accumulated wealth.

Trustee

A person or corporation named in a trust agreement who is acting in a fiduciary capacity for the benefit of the grantor and the grantor's trust beneficiaries. The trustee is responsible for holding, managing, investing, accounting for, and distributing property from the trust to the trust beneficiaries.

Trust Protector

A term originating from English common law that refers to a "watch dog," being a person or corporation who has certain powers such as the ability to hire or fire trustees, to veto trust distributions or to add new beneficiaries. Trust protectors are routinely used in all domestic and offshore asset protection trusts as well as in many irrevocable trusts such as life insurance trusts.

Uniform Fraudulent Transfer Act (UFTA)

Adopted in 1984 to replace the Uniform Fraudulent Conveyances Act, The Uniform Fraudulent Transfer Act provides uniform penalties in many states against debtors who fraudulently transfer assets to avoid creditors.

Unified Credit Exemption

More properly referred to as the "applicable exemption amount" which is the amount of assets that can pass without imposition of an estate tax or gift tax on the transfer. The federal gift tax exemption is $1,000,000 and not scheduled to increase at any time during an entire period of time.

Variable Annuity

A type of annuity where the account balance fluctuates in accordance with the underlying investments. The contract owner, not the insurance company, is responsible for making the investment decisions.

Will or Last Will and Testament

A formal written document by which a person who is over the age of eighteen (18) may direct the disposition of their personal and real property after death. Wills are used to name legal guardians for minor children and to name personal representatives or executors. When a person dies without having properly prepared their last will and testament, the distribution of their estate will be made in accordance with the default rules of the state in which they were residing, which rules are referred to as the "laws of intestacy". These laws completely govern who receives how much of that person's estate regardless of what the decedent may have desired.